Workplace Etiquette

A Guide to Surviving and Thriving in Today's Workplace

(What You *Don't* Know *Could* Hurt Your Career Success!)

by Dianne Floyd Sutton

Love and Peace
Dianne Floyd Sutton

Sutton Enterprises Press

Workplace Etiquette
A Guide to Surviving and Thriving in Today's Workplace

By Dianne Floyd Sutton

Copyright © 2004 by Sutton Enterprises
First printing: March 2005 as ISBN: 1-891962-26-4
Published October 2009 as ISBN 978-0-9823831-0-0

Published by
Sutton Enterprises Press
Kensington, Maryland
Phone: (301) 585-1446
SEImpact@aol.com

The Political Savvy Quiz and Tips are the work of Tim Stranges of The Timothy Group, who has given his permission for their inclusion in this book.

Printed in the USA

CONTENTS

Acknowledgments

This book was created through the unconditional love and support of many people in my personal and professional life. I was blessed to be inspired, challenged, and supported by the wisdom and caring of many. I must thank a few people publicly for their unwavering faith and nurturing during the creation of this publication.

First my aunt, Delores Finley, who is a retired educator and artist in Denver, Colorado. Her insight and encouragement motivated me to continue this project. Aunt Dee is a grand dame of etiquette.

I could not have proceeded at all without the knowledge and skills of Tim Stranges of the The Timothy Group in Rockville, Maryland. Tim not only contributed his own work on political savvy but continuously helped me throughout this process. He was always cheerful – reading and editing and reediting numerous drafts.

Special thanks to Tony Stubbs, editor, for his clear-headed and genuine enthusiasm. He patiently worked with me while I earned a living.

Over five years ago, It dawned on me that some employees had no clue about what was really expected of them in the workplace or what they needed to get ahead in the continuously changing world of work. This book originated as a workshop design to help individuals understand the written and unwritten rules regarding etiquette, professional presence, and political savvy. Special thanks to the National Science Foundation (NSF) in Washington, D.C., for allowing me to pilot my workshop on office professionalism at their facility for their employees. As a result of the NSF experience, I realized that a vast audience of people need this information. Thus, this book, *Workplace Etiquette,* was created as a basic toolkit to help others survive and thrive in today's workplace.

The truth is: what you *don't* know *could* hurt your career success!

About the Author

Dianne Floyd Sutton is President of Sutton Enterprises, author, workshop designer, trainer, educator, expert witness, life coach, and actor. She has over twenty years of experience in Human Resource Development (HRD) and Equal Employment Opportunity (EEO) training. She also taught parttime at the American University School of Communication in Washington, D.C. for twelve years.

Through her combined HRD and EEO experiences, Ms. Sutton has developed skills and processes that enhance personal, team, and organizational development and productivity. She has designed, delivered, and facilitated courses, workshops, and retreats for thousands of people on such topics as leadership, conflict resolution, people management, positive self-esteem, interpersonal and group communication, sexual harassment, and diversity and cultural competency.

Her publications include *Managing Your Starship: Multicultural Management for the Twenty-First Century, Recovering Your Lost Self,* and *How Do You Define Yourself?* When you combine real-life solutions with a dynamic personality, humor, and boundless energy, you have Dianne Floyd Sutton. She knows exactly how to relate to the challenges that people face in today's workforce. Ms. Sutton develops and delivers programs that help individuals strengthen communication, reduce stress, and overcome conflict.

Preface

Why write a book on the topic of workplace etiquette?

In the world of work, we are still judged by how we look and conduct ourselves around others. Although the workplace diversity movement emphasizes inclusion and respect, some constant, subtle behavioral expectations are frequently overlooked or unknown by employees. They are the written and unwritten rules of etiquette.

Why is etiquette so important? Because people judge you and your organization by what they see and what they believe to be true. If they perceive that you're even slightly crude, rude, uncultured, or unrefined, your career or business may suffer. If people perceive you to be a knowledgeable, smooth professional, they'll want to work with and do business with you.

Workplace etiquette generates confidence, helps to eliminate distractions, and creates a pleasant environment in which people can work to their full potential. Professional manners may not be listed in your job description, but they certainly play a critical part in your career. The ability to handle yourself properly outweighs even your technical skills. If you know what to do, when to do it, and how to do it with grace and style, you'll have a competitive edge in your career. Good manners mean good business.

Many rules of work behavior and professional interaction have changed. Fast-paced, evolving technological advances have altered organizational culture. The basic principles of etiquette, even those that are evolving, are valuable, specific, and accessible. Understand that cultural norms differ; that behavioral expectations differ not only from one culture to another but also from region to region, industry to industry, and even office to office. Despite these variations, there remains a core of U.S. business etiquette behaviors that transcend the minor differences in style and that can quickly become a minefield if ignored.

Career politics goes beyond office professionalism to focus on such important topics as building relationships, networking, and team building. It provides you with the information you need to make the right decisions to advance your career.

You never get a second chance to make a good first impression, and you make first impressions every day. You succeed or fail by the impressions you create in briefings, interviews, phone calls, sales meetings, conflict resolutions, and the countless encounters of everyday work life.

In the fast pace of a workday, deals can be won or lost, careers made or destroyed, and relationships established or broken – all in a matter of minutes. Indeed, in face-to-face encounters, you typically get only two to four minutes. On the telephone, you have just seconds. During your first few minutes of interaction with others, their attention span is at its greatest and their powers of retention highest. Their eyes and ears focus on you and tell their brains what they see and hear. A negative impression may be difficult, perhaps impossible, to change.

This workbook introduces you to the basic knowledge and skills you need to conduct yourself effectively, correctly, and confidently in most work environments, professional situations, and business social settings. It is not hard, mystical, or complicated – it takes only a mindset and practice.

Objectives of This Book

The objectives of this book are to help you:

1. Understand the importance of observing codes of conduct and other written rules that govern behavior in organizations

2. Understand the importance of observing unwritten rules of conduct and work-place etiquette

3. Understand factors that people notice when meeting you

4. Learn and practice basic etiquette rules

5. Realize you have choices in how you conduct yourself in the workplace and understand that your choices may influence how you are perceived by your coworkers and may determine how far your career progresses.

Personal Objectives

Write your personal objectives for reading this book.

1. Body Piercings and Tattoos

2. Networking

3.

4.

5.

After Reading This Book

After you have read the book, review your objectives. Did you meet them? If not, why not?

How This Book is Organized

This book is organized into chapters by specific topics. You don't need to read a previous chapter to understand the one that interests you, but it may improve your overall understanding of what workplace etiquette means. What makes this guidebook unique is that each chapter includes an activity (exercise, drill, personal assessment, or quiz) to reinforce the material presented. The following is a description of each chapter and what you can expect to find in it.

Chapter 1: Introduction – This chapter begins with a quiz that allows you to assess what you already know about workplace etiquette. It defines terms such as etiquette and professional presence and also examines the concept of culture in your personal and work world.

Activities:

- What Do You Know Before You Begin? - A Quiz
- Comparing Personal and Organizational Culture
- Organizational Culture - Written Rules vs. Unwritten Rules

Chapter 2: Etiquette Basics – What is appropriate social behavior in everyday interactions? This chapter gives guidelines on acceptable behavior and also tips on interacting with disabled individuals.

Activity:

- Etiquette Quiz

Chapter 3: Introductions and Small Talk – This chapter gives guidance on effectively greeting others in the workplace. It includes tips on shaking hands and using small talk.

Activities:

- Practicing Introductions
- Meeting and Greeting Quiz
- Introducing Yourself

Chapter 4: Business Dress and Grooming – The importance of appearance in establishing a professional image cannot be over-stressed. This chapter discusses the importance of a professional appearance. It examines what is and what is not appropriate dress and grooming.

Activity:

- Checking Out Your Role Model

Chapter 5: Dining Etiquette – Table manners play an important role in making a favorable impression. This chapter gives guidance on appropriate dining manners.

Activity:

- Dining Quiz

Chapter 6: Nonverbal Communication – Body language is as important as spoken language. This chapter gives tips on how to use body language to improve communication skills.

Activities:

- Who Do You Touch?
- Assessing Your Appearance
- Nonverbal Feedback

Chapter 7: Verbal Communication – Your voice can be an asset or liability. The voice you project is determined by factors you can control. This chapter gives tips and drills to enhance your speaking ability.

Activities:

- Listening to the Sound of Your Voice
- Speech Exercises
- Practice Drills for Polishing Your Speaking Voice

Chapter 8: Electronic Communication – This chapter gives tips on how to project a professional image via email and telephone.

Activity:

- Telephone Quiz

Chapter 9: Political Savvy – It is difficult to progress in your career without engaging in some form of office politics. This chapter gives tools and techniques for playing effective politics in the workplace.

Activities:

- Identify Your Hot Buttons
- Political Savvy Quiz
- Identifying Your Networks

Please note that many additional topics could have been included in this book. The result, however, would have been overwhelming and awfully thick. If you learn how to enhance your professional presence after reading this book, then you will be ready for the next installment.

Chapter 1

INTRODUCTION

1. status talk

2. First / Last name

3. make job sound exciting

4. Performance, Image, exposure
       10%   30%   60%

5. Tom Peters - brand called you → Google

INTRODUCTION

Exercise – What Do You Know Before We Begin? - A Quiz*

Directions: For each statement, circle either T for True or F for False

T	F	1.	If you are asked to pass the bread or rolls, always pass the butter too without being asked.
T	F	2.	The person with the highest rank in business is always mentioned first in an introduction. Gender is not a consideration.
T	F	3.	In an office setting, select the arm chair, not the sofa.
T	F	4.	Every industry has its own wardrobe requirements. One standard does not fit everyone.
T	F	5.	A man should wait for a woman in business to offer her hand in greeting.
T	F	6.	As you eat, use your silverware from the inside out.
T	F	7.	Showing cleavage is appropriate in most work environments.
T	F	8.	The use of silence is a powerful way to establish presence.
T	F	9.	Beautiful teeth project an image of good breeding and good health.
T	F	10.	If you are served before others in your group, start eating before your food gets cold.
T	F	11.	The general rule of table setting is liquids on your right and solids on your left.
T	F	12.	Sit as close to the leader as protocol permits.
T	F	13.	Standing up while on the phone will enhance the quality of your voice.
T	F	14.	Intimidation works when all else fails.
T	F	15.	It is impossible to be considered sophisticated without a working knowledge of basic etiquette.
T	F	16.	Creating a calm presence is particularly important when you have made a severe social mistake.
T	F	17.	Don't associate yourself with negative employees, because you will become viewed as negative by association.
T	F	18.	It's okay to use someone else's idea and take credit.
T	F	19.	If you and your supervisor have a disagreement, it's okay to go over their head without telling them.
T	F	20.	"Business casual" attire has the emphasis more on business than on casual.
T	F	21.	Community involvement is part of having professional presence.
T	F	22.	It is easier to influence others and exert status in person than by telephone, fax, or email.
T	F	23.	It is difficult to move forward in any organization without engaging in some form of office politics.
T	F	24.	If you have tattoos on your arms, it's fine to wear short-sleeved or sleeveless shirts/blouses to show them off at work.
T	F	25.	A confident statement can be negated by weak body language.
T	F	26.	Your napkin is the one on the left.
T	F	27.	Exchange business cards at the beginning of the meeting.

* Adapted from *Professional Presence* by Susan Bixler, "What Is Your Professional Presence Quotient?"

Quiz (continued)

T	F	28.	It's okay to talk on your cell phone at the dining table.
T	F	29.	When shaking hands, "pump" the person's hand once or twice (about as long as it takes to say both names), but don't continue to hold on. Even if your introduction continues, let go of their hand.
T	F	30.	When you are upset, it is possible to communicate a negative attitude over the phone without realizing it.
T	F	31.	Your nonverbal communication often speaks louder than your words.
T	F	32.	If you want the job, you have to look the part.
T	F	33.	In the USA, a firm handshake shows confidence, warmth, openness, and sincerity; a weak, limp handshake shows just the opposite.
T	F	34.	Don't miss your boss's big speech at the big event.
T	F	35.	Eating something before a business event is considered smart if you have a large appetite.
T	F	36.	Someone has just walked up to you and introduced himself, but you weren't listening very well and didn't get his name. You don't ask again because you don't want to look stupid. This is fine.
T	F	37.	Scoop your soup toward you.
T	F	38.	As long as you apologize, you can reach over the dining table.
T	F	39.	Bring food to your mouth, not your mouth to the food.
T	F	40.	As long as you do a good job, it does not matter how you package yourself.
T	F	41.	When using email, include the topic of your message in the subject area.
T	F	42.	Never help out anyone if it doesn't benefit your job.
T	F	43.	At a business lunch, because time is limited, begin business discussions as soon as you sit down.
T	F	44.	Professional presence is comprised of all the resources that you have to influence others.
T	F	45.	An important characteristic of showing power and presence is the ability to put others at ease while appearing comfortable yourself.
T	F	46.	Don't season your food before tasting it.
T	F	47.	Appearance includes much more than dress or clothing.
T	F	48.	In business, start with direct eye contact as your point of reference and adjust from there.
T	F	49.	When meeting a person who is blind/visually impaired, always identify yourself and others who may be with you.
T	F	50.	Your food will be served from the right, so expect the server to reach over your shoulder.

After taking this quiz, check your responses against the answers on page 92.

- I have a can do attitude - go getter
- Golden child - bosses pet

- no
- Dedicated Hard worker, Team player, Respected, someone that they can go to for service

Attitude is Your Key to Success!
Or: If you think you will succeed, you will!

- Your attitude toward your life influences your behavior.
- Your attitude determines the level of your job satisfaction and professionalism.
- Your attitude affects everyone who comes in contact with you, either in person or on the telephone.
- Your attitude is not only reflected by your tone of voice but also by the way you stand or sit, your facial expression, and in other nonverbal ways.
- Your attitude is not fixed. The attitude you choose to display is up to you.
- Remember that no one is ever rewarded or promoted because of a bad disposition or negative attitude.
- If you have more enemies than friends, it is time to examine your attitude.
- Remember, your mental limitations are of your own making.
- It is not defeat, but rather your attitude toward it, that whips you.
- Your attitude is your real boss.
- Change your attitude, and the world around you will change accordingly.

Have you ever heard of a self-fulfilling prophecy? It often happens without our conscious awareness of it. Self-fulfilling prophecy is the phenomenon that results when we experience what we *expect* to experience. It is our getting from others just what we thought we would. We often succeed or fail because we subconsciously "knew" we would!

Our lives are full of examples of this phenomenon. Have you ever thought, "I'll never get this finished on time!" and then proved yourself right? Have you noticed that some people approach situations with an "I can't do this" attitude and experience problems and failures, while others approach the same situations with an "I can do this" attitude and succeed? Expectations and attitudes are powerful influences on actual outcomes. Your mind is one of the most powerful forces on earth. It can be your strongest ally or your worst enemy. How often have you imagined failure and fulfilled that negative expectation? What would happen if you put as much creativity and emotional energy into picturing success?

The longer I live, the more I realize the impact of attitude on life. Attitude, to me, is more important than circumstances.

The remarkable thing is we have a choice to make every day regarding the attitude we will embrace for that day. We cannot change our past, nor can we change the fact that people will behave in a certain way. The only thing we can do is change our attitude. The longer you live, the more you will realize the impact of attitude on your life.

> "I am convinced that life is 10% what happens to me and 90% how I react to it. And so it is with you ... we are in charge of our attitudes."
> ~ *Charles Swindoll*, pastor of the First Evangelical Free Church of Fullerton, California, and an avid proponent of new evangelicalism.

What is Etiquette? *- BASED ON culture of Organization*

- Conventional requirements regarding proper social behavior
- Manners, courtesy, civility, politeness, social graces
- Behaving a little better than is absolutely essential
- The ability to handle yourself properly
- Etiquette relies on tradition, social expectations, and behavioral standards, all of which are based on understanding, kindness, courtesy, efficiency, and common sense

---

Etiquette comes from the French. Originally it meant a solder's billet for lodgings, then an identification label or ticket. Later, the word came to designate the complex body of ceremonial rules governing the royal court of France. Finally it entered the English language about 1750 with its present meaning: the customary rules of conduct in a civilized society.

— *The Manager's Pocket Guide to Emotional Intelligence,*
Emily A. Sterett, Ph.D. (HRD Press, Amherst, MA, 2000)

What is Business Etiquette?

Webster's New World Dictionary defines etiquette as "the forms, manners, and ceremonies established by convention as acceptable or required in social relations, in a profession, or in official life." Business etiquette, then, is the way professional business people—no matter what their job title or type of business—conduct themselves around others. By definition, business etiquette is a set of rules that allows us to communicate and interact in a civilized manner. It is more than just good manners in the workplace. Business etiquette involves the rules, mores, procedures, and manners that are required in a profession or workplace.

As we become a more high-tech society, the need for a sensitive, personal touch in organizations increases. No matter how intelligent or accurate your computer is, you must still interact with other people. When you use accepted etiquette, you're using the behaviors that encourage a positive human response. You're more likely to earn cooperation and support, get commitments, gain customers, and keep peace. Those people you depend on in a pinch will usually come through for you. You are more likely to succeed when you consistently put that something extra into your way of doing business.

Professional Presence

- Professional presence is the ability to project a sense of poise or self-assurance in the workplace.
- Professional presence enables you to act in any situation with a clear advantage, without making other people feel uncomfortable.
- Professional presence is comprised of all the resources you have to influence others.
- Professional presence is a mature recognition that tact and diplomacy go hand-in-hand and that far more can be negotiated than forced.
- Professional presence is the way you present yourself in the workplace that creates power, credibility, and a sense of competence.
- Professional presence affects your promotability, your effectiveness as a leader, your effectiveness with coworkers, and how management perceives you.

Notes:

1. An important characteristic of showing power and presence is the ability to put others at ease while appearing comfortable yourself.
2. A golden rule of professional presence is never to make anyone feel embarrassed or make the embarrassment greater than it already is.

Tact and Diplomacy

Tact is defined as a keen sense of what to say or do to avoid giving offense; a knowledge of what is appropriate and tasteful.

Diplomacy is the skill of managing negotiations and handling people so that little or no ill will results.

Remember: Any time you violate the expectations of the dress code in your occupation or the degree of formality at a public ceremony or event, you assume risks. With those risks may come consequences, not the least of which may be a negative first impression.

Culture and Cross-Cultural Misinterpretations

- Culture is everything that an individual learns from the various members of society (family, friends, school, religious training, media, books, etc.).

- Culture is shared values, beliefs, language, traditions, world views, guidelines, symbols, and stories.

- Culture is the basis for what/who is considered good, bad, or important in a society.

- Culture is reinforced consciously and unconsciously.

- Culture is a society's non-debatable, taken-for-granted basic assumptions.

Culture Tells Us ...

1. What is Real
(perception)

2. What is Good
(values)

3. What to Do
(behavior)

Misunderstandings sometimes occur when a meaning that exists in one culture results in a different interpretation of behavior or events in another culture. People tend to see their own way of life as the right and natural way and often are amused or revolted by other people's customs.

Examples:

- Physical distance between people

- Expressions of conflict

- Demonstrations of respect

- Regard for time

- Eye contact

- Diet and eating habits

- Expressions of love

Organizational Culture is:

The written and unwritten rules of behavior for employees in an organization.

1. What you say and do
2. Who you say it to
3. When you say it
4. Why you say it
5. How you say it and do it

Every office has a unique culture that addresses issues of time, dress, formality, chain of command, etc. For example, in some offices, if a meeting is called for 10:00 a.m., it starts at 10:00 a.m. In other offices, the same meeting will start at 10:05 a.m. or later. If you want to succeed in your organization, you must understand and abide by all the aspects of its culture.

Exercise – Comparing Personal and Organizational Cultures

Take a moment to compare your personal culture (behaviors, etc., away from work) with the culture of your organization. Are there differences? Do you need to make cultural adjustments when at work?

	My Personal Culture	My Organization's Culture	
1. Space/Physical Closeness	Same		Hand Shake
2. Time/Punctuality/ Tardiness	Ahead of Schedule or on Time w/ work requirement	laid back Approach until requirements outside of organization – Priority	30 mins Prior
3. Dress/Grooming	Business Casual Casual	laid back Boss – GI3 Jeans Sweats	Dress to Industry Be conservative
4. Degree of Formality/ Familiarity			
5. Respect	same		
6. Greeting/Leave-Taking		Nosey –	
7. Patterns of Conversation	one person talk at a Time	Talk over one another	
8. Conflict Resolution	Deal with it	ignore it	Relate problem to productivity

If you decide to make a personal statement by disregarding your organization's cultural standards, be very sure that you know what you are doing and why you are doing it. Try to succeed at fitting in before you try to stand out. Also, be alert to the special sensitivities and needs of your coworkers. As diversity in the workplace brings together many people from different ethnic, social, cultural, and religious backgrounds, you need to have a much more tolerant and inclusive attitude at work than you would at home within your own culture.

Exercise: Organizational Culture

The Written Rules of Conduct in Your Organization

What are the written rules found in your employee handbook and/or code of conduct? For example: "All employees must come to work at 8:00 a.m. and leave at 4:30 p.m."

The Unwritten Rules of Conduct in Your Organization

What rules are not written down—i.e., rules that you learn from co-workers, mentors, and/or coaches—that are essential for succeeding in your organization? For example: "Even though you may come to work at 8:00 a.m., if there is an important project due, you must stay late to help the boss."

Chapter 2

ETIQUETTE BASICS

ETIQUETTE BASICS

Holding Doors Open

Opening doors for others is simply a physical recognition of the dignity of another. If people of the same gender approach a door together, the one in the higher position or the one considerably older usually enters first, while the other person typically holds the door for them. Just remember that common sense rules. If someone is carrying an armful of files or packages, the other person takes the lead in all situations regardless of sex, age, or position. Assistance should be given to persons with a disability. Doors should also be opened and held for customers and clients.

Public Transportation Etiquette

What about the rule that men or younger people must give up their seats on a bus, train, or subway to women or older people? Not any more — unless the people are disabled, pregnant, or elderly. Of course, offering your seat is still a nice gesture. When riding on escalators and people-movers, stand on the right and pass on the left. This also applies to walking on public sidewalks and in hallways.

Elevator Etiquette

Common sense dictates that the people closest to the elevator doors get on first. If you want to be at the front when it's time to get out, go in and stand by the buttons, out of the way. Don't stand around to see who else is leaving. If you're in the very front waiting for your floor, move outside of the doors to allow people to exit from the back. Consideration of the entire group should always come before consideration of one person, especially in an elevator.

Street Etiquette

There is an old rule that a man has to walk on the street side of the curb. This rule came into being during the days before paved streets, when mud was everywhere and garbage and waste were still being thrown out of open windows overhead. Men were supposed to be gallant enough to let their clothes get dirty rather than allow their female companion's clothes to become soiled. Today it's not necessary or practical to walk along a busy street changing sides every few blocks just to make sure the man stays on the street side, nor must a man offer his arm to a woman as they walk.

Common Courtesies

- Saying "Please," "Thank you," "Excuse me," "Pardon me," and "May I"

- Asking someone to be seated

- Showing a visitor or guest to a door

- Holding the door for someone behind you

- Writing, not e-mailing, thank-you notes promptly

- Acknowledging other people as they walk past you

Ten Commandments for Good Manners (by Larry G. Evans)

Reproduced with permission from www.bixxo.com/npa/10_com.html

1. Thou Shalt Be Thyself.

Good manners begin with a good sense of self. Unless you are true to yourself, you can never be true to others. You are unique. Don't try to shape your personality to meet circumstances. Be natural, and the world will respect you for what you are.

2. Thou Shalt Say "Thank You."

Thanking others is a way of praising them and is one of the keys to having good manners. Send thank-you notes whenever someone does something nice for you, or telephone to express your gratitude. This simple act will help build lasting relationships. When someone gives you a compliment, the best response is a simple "thank you." And don't forget "Please," "Excuse me," and "You're welcome," which are other marks of good manners.

3. Thou Shalt Give Compliments.

A fundamental rule of good manners is to give. Think about what you can give to others, and remember that the most precious gifts cost nothing. When you meet someone, you can always think of a genuine compliment to give. A "Hello" or "How are you?" is not enough. You can also give your undivided attention and interest to others. You can be generous with words of praise, warm greetings, sympathy, love, or other good news.

4. Thou Shalt Not be Boastful, Arrogant, or Loud.

Always exercise restraint and good taste. Your voice, your behavior and even your clothing should reflect understated elegance. Only a small person brags about accomplishments; a well-mannered person has no need for self-advertisement. Let your deeds speak for themselves.

5. Thou Shalt Listen Before Speaking.

Respect for others is a prerequisite of good manners. Listening to others is a way to show respect. There is no worse company than a person who does not listen. Be genuinely interested in others; learn their names and encourage them to talk about themselves. Never interrupt. Look them in the eye and listen carefully. The listener learns and thereby gains.

6. Thou Shalt Speak with Kindness and Caution.

Before speaking to others, consider what effect your words will have. Pause and weigh your words carefully and say them with a quality of softness. A slip of the tongue can inflict needless hurt. Also, remember the language of the body (your posture and your mannerisms) is as important as the language of words.

7. Thou Shalt Not Criticize or Complain.

A person with good manners is above criticizing others or complaining about circumstances. Negativity in any form is to be avoided. If you hear gossip, don't join in; be indifferent to it. If you disagree with others, do so respectfully. Don't verbally attack or condemn them. You may win the argument but lose a valued friend.

8. Thou Shalt Be Punctual.

Appreciate the value of time, yours and others. If you make an appointment, arrive on time. If you must be late, call first. Never arrive early for a social engagement; your host may still be getting dressed! Don't overstay your welcome. Lingering good-byes merely cause frustration and can ruin an otherwise good time. A quick, simple exit at the proper time is usually appreciated.

9. Thou Shalt Not Embarrass Others.

Treat others as you would like to be treated and think of how you can put them at ease. The feelings of other people can be as fragile as fine crystal. Never demean anyone with rude jokes or an unwelcome nickname. Be considerate. In conversation, never ask embarrassing questions such as how much was paid for a new item or about matters of the heart. It's always good manners to think of others first.

10. Thou Shalt Act and Look Your Best.

A gracious friend is never ruffled. Be a calming, happy influence in any stressful situation and maintain your composure. See humor whenever possible. Master self-control and have empathy for others. Always act your best with courtesy and politeness. Each day, dress as if it were your only chance to shine. A smile should top your list of accessories. Your home, car, and workplace should reflect your best. They should be tidy, neat, and well organized. Table manners are important. Observe rules of proper conduct such as not speaking with food in your mouth and not eating until the host has been seated. Eat slowly, enjoying each bite. Savor the moments when good friends, good conversation, and good manners bring about the best life has to offer.

Memo

Negative Gestures to Avoid

- Checking your watch
- Interrupting
- Cracking knuckles
- Pointing
- Backslapping
- Staring
- Using toothpicks in public
- Whispering
- Chewing gum in public
- Walking in front of someone
- Laughing too loudly
- Burping
- Scratching the private parts of your body

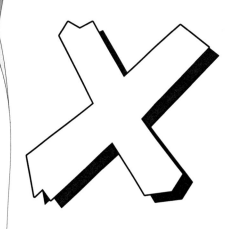

Dealing with Biological Functions

- Always carry a handkerchief or a small package of tissues. Reach for them at the first hint of a sneeze coming on.

- Forestall a sneeze at a critical moment by pressing your extended index finger flat and firmly against your upper lip, just under your nostrils. This works temporarily.

- Sneeze gently. Practice sneezing without vocalizing.

- When you sneeze, turn from those close at hand. When seated, try to bend toward the floor.

- If a sneezing fit seizes you, excuse yourself from the room.

- If you feel a belch coming on, use your napkin to cover your mouth, turn away from others, and do it quietly.

- If you feel any other gas passing, excuse yourself immediately from the room until your digestive system calms down.

- If you are speaking to someone and you belch unexpectedly, say "Excuse me" and go right on with your conversation. Any statement you make in an attempt to mitigate the belch will only make it worse.

Smoking   *smoking kit   mints, Febreeze*

The etiquette of smoking today is simple. Don't do it in front of other people. It used to be a shared experience—meeting over a cup of coffee and a cigarette—but no more. Smoking in public is almost like using a toothpick: it is best done alone or with other smokers.

Smoking No - No's

- If you don't see an ashtray, don't smoke.

- Never smoke in someone's car.

- Don't smoke in a restaurant, even in the smoking section, unless everyone else is smoking at your table.

- Don't smoke in a client's office, even if they are doing so.

- Don't smoke in your own car if you are heading to an important appointment. The smell will linger on your clothes and could make a bad impression.

- Don't wear the same suit the day after you have gone to a smoky bar.

- When all else fails, use common sense. If you must light up, excuse yourself and go outside.

Thank-You Notes   ~Dollar Store~

Thank-you notes are incredibly valuable for establishing professional presence because so few people take the time to write them. Do not use the fax or e-mail to send a thank-you note. Either write it out or type it.

Use only black or navy blue ink for your handwritten notes.

Thank-you notes are appropriate for:

- After a job interview, to people at home and/or work who helped you get in or get through the interview
- After signing or not signing a big contract
- Any gift given to you
- Any favor done for you - ~Captain/Susan~

Use the other person's first name in the note, except for a thank-you after a job interview. Include one or two lines about why their assistance or quality was important to you, and one or two lines about what your relationship means to you. Finally, close by signing your first name.

People with Disabilities are Just Like Everyone Else

Remember that people with disabilities are like everyone else — except they happen to have a disability. Here are a few tips for improving your language related to disabilities and handicaps.

1. Speak of the person first, then the disability.
2. Emphasize abilities, not limitations.
3. Do not label people as part of a disability group — don't say "the disabled"; say "people with disabilities."
4. Don't give excessive praise or attention to a person with a disability; don't patronize them.
5. Choice and independence are important; let the person do or speak for him/herself as much as possible.
6. A disability is a functional limitation that interferes with a person's ability to walk, hear, talk, learn, etc. Use "handicap" to describe a situation or barrier imposed by society, the environment, or oneself.

Etiquette for Communicating with People with Disabilities

1. When talking with a person with a disability, speak directly to that person rather than through a companion or sign-language interpreter.

2. When introduced to a person with a disability, it is appropriate to offer to shake hands. People with limited hand use or who wear an artificial limb can usually shake hands. (Shaking hands with the left hand is an acceptable greeting.)

3. When meeting a person who is blind/visually impaired, always identify yourself and others who may be with you. When conversing in a group, remember to identify the person to whom you are speaking.

4. If you offer assistance, wait until the offer is accepted before proceeding. Then listen to or ask for instructions.

5. Treat adults as adults. Address people who have disabilities by their first names only when extending the same familiarity to all others. (Never patronize people who use wheelchairs by patting them on the head or shoulder.)

6. Leaning on or hanging on to a person's wheelchair is similar to leaning or hanging on to a person and is generally considered annoying. The chair is part of the personal body space of the person who uses it.

7. Listen attentively when you're talking with a person who has difficulty speaking. Be patient and wait for the person to finish, rather than correcting or speaking for the person. If necessary, ask short questions that require short answers, a nod, or shake of the head. Never pretend to understand if you are having difficulty doing so. Instead, repeat what you have understood and allow the person to respond. The response will clue you in and guide your understanding.

8. When speaking with a person who uses a wheelchair or a person who uses crutches, place yourself at eye level in front of the person to facilitate the conversation.

9. To get the attention of a person who is deaf/hearing impaired, tap the person on the shoulder or wave your hand. Look directly at the person and speak clearly, slowly, and expressively to determine if the person can read your lips. Not all people who are deaf can read lips. For those who do lip read, be sensitive to their needs by placing yourself so that you face the light source and keep hands and food away from your mouth when speaking.

10. Don't be embarrassed if you happen to use accepted, common expressions such as "See you later," or "Did you hear about that?" that seem to relate to a person's disability. Don't be afraid to ask questions when you're unsure of what to do.

Communication

Acts of Rudeness

1. Being late

2. Talking over someone

3. Disrespecting someone ideas

4. not doing what you say

5. Degrading someone in public

6. No saying hello when spoken to

7. cutting someone off during conversation
no listening

8. ~~Footba~~

9. in my space — sitting on Desk

10. not shaking hands during greetings

Jokes and Off-Color Humor

Never feel pressured to behave like rude, impolite coworkers just to fit in at work. You don't have to pretend to be amused by vulgar language, sexual/off-color jokes or jokes made at the expense of others. Topics not to joke about at work include:

Race	Gender	Sexual Orientation	Religion
Age	Ethnicity	Marital Status	Disabilities

Exercise – Etiquette Basics Quiz

Directions: Circle either T for True or F for False

T	F	1.	Listening is a way to show respect.
T	F	2.	If you are in the very front of the elevator waiting for your floor, move outside of the elevator doors to allow people to exit from the back.
T	F	3.	If you belch unexpectedly while talking to someone, say "Excuse me" and go right on with your conversation.
T	F	4.	If you offer assistance to an individual who is disabled, wait until the offer is accepted before proceeding.
T	F	5.	Avoid using a toothpick in public.
T	F	6.	Thank-you notes should be written and not e-mailed.
T	F	7.	You should hold the door open for someone who is older than you.
T	F	8.	When meeting a person who is blind/visually impaired, always identify yourself.
T	F	9.	When riding on the escalators stand on the right and pass on the left.
T	F	10.	If you don't see an ashtray, just ask.

(Answers on page 92)

Chapter 3

INTRODUCTIONS AND SMALL TALK

INTRODUCTIONS AND SMALL TALK

Shaking Hands

The way you greet others — not only by what you say, but by your body language — tells a lot about you. Meeting others in a pleasant way and showing sincere interest in them helps produce a favorable first impression.

1. Shaking hands is the most established form of etiquette in the U.S. today. It began as a sign of peace — proving that you weren't carrying a concealed weapon — and it remains a peaceable gesture. More than that, most people consider it an insult if you refuse to shake hands, regardless of your culture.

2. If you can't shake with your right hand for some reason, offer your left hand. If your disability is permanent, you needn't apologize for it. If it's temporary, you need only smile and say something like, "My right hand's a little under the weather right now." You don't have to explain your entire accident. If someone asks, make your explanation short and simple.

3. Your handshake says a lot about you. A firm handshake shows confidence, warmth, openness, and sincerity; a weak, limp handshake indicates just the opposite. A bone-crusher hand shake tells people you're a dominating, insensitive type.

4. "Pump" the person's hand once or twice (about as long as it takes to say both names), but don't continue to hold on. Even if your introduction continues, let go of their hand. Lean forward slightly during the handshake, smile, and make direct eye contact. In the U.S., a handshake without direct eye contact suggests hesitancy, untruthfulness, or a feeling of inferiority.

5. When you shake hands, keep your hand straight, thumb knuckle facing upward. When people turn their hand so their palm faces down in the handshake, it transmits an unconscious feeling of dominance. You appear submissive if you allow the other person's hand to take the dominant position.

6. In business situations, never double-clasp (put your left hand over their right hand), put your arm around someone's neck, put your hand on their shoulder, kiss (or air-kiss) their cheeks, or touch them in any other way (except their hand). Be respectful of their personality style; not everyone feels comfortable with touching. Hugging and kissing are definite no-nos in the office setting, no matter how friendly your group or how close you feel to someone.

7. There was a time when the rules of etiquette dictated that a man should wait for a woman to offer her hand first in greeting. No longer. Equality governs today; both parties typically extend their hands at the same time. Even rivals are expected to forgo their competition long enough to perform this small courtesy.

8. What do you do if you extend your hand and the other person doesn't take it? Simply withdraw your hand discreetly, don't comment, and don't feel any shame or embarrassment.

NOTES

Handshakes

- Shake hands crisply and firmly.
- Meet web to web, and don't pump up and down more than once.
- Don't sandwich the other person's hand between both of yours.
- Don't "bone crush" the other person's hand.
- Don't give a limp, dead-fish shake.
- When shaking hands, treat men and women with equal respect.
- It is as appropriate for a man to offer his hand to a woman in greeting as it is for her to offer first. Gender is not a consideration.
- Traditionally, women have either nodded to each other in greeting or hugged one another. But in business situations, a firm handshake is the appropriate greeting.

Three Handshake Positions

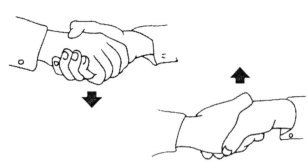

Taking Control (Wrong)   Giving Control (Wrong)   Shaking Like a Professional (Right)

Introducing People

Although we business people may not be as formal as we used to be, introductions are still very important. When you introduce someone, start with "Ms. Long, meet Mr. Roscoe from Company/Department/State," or "Mrs. Brown, I'd like to introduce my son, Cliff. Cliff, this is Mrs. Brown." Never phrase an introduction as a command: "Mr. Roscoe, shake hands with Ms. Long."

Refrain from long stories about how you met the person you're introducing, or about the person's life or background. Avoid phrases of superiority like "Jeff works for me" or "Sally is our Girl Friday."

Titles

Because so much of business/corporate culture is based on rank and status, titles are vitally important. In the company of others, especially with people outside your organization, show your supervisor and/or manager respect by addressing him or her formally as "Mr. Smith" or "Ms. Johnson."

"Ms." is the appropriate address for a woman in business, regardless of what she chooses to call herself in her private life. "Mrs." and "Miss" imply social and marital distinctions that should not have any importance in the business area.

Of course, if a woman tells you directly that she wishes to be addressed as "Mrs." or "Miss," it is best to comply. However, when using "Mrs." in a business context, use the woman's first name rather than her husband's. For example, "Mrs. Jean Smith."

Always present the older person, guest of honor, or dignitary first. Be sure to use titles, not first names, when introducing a much older person, a doctor (i.e., physician, psychologist, veterinarian, or Ph.D.), a member of the clergy, or someone of official rank.

Use the dignitary's title even if that person is retired or no longer holds that position (e.g., "Governor Brown," "Mayor Taylor," "Colonel Johnson," "Ambassador Smith").

Proper Introductions

When Introducing:	Name to Say First:
Younger person to older person (Use youngster's first name, older person's last — about 15 years is the deciding point.)	Older person's ("Ms. Sutton, this is Johnny Alexander.")
Peer in your organization to outsider	Outsider's
Nonofficial to official	Official's
Junior executive to senior executive	Senior Executive's
Company executive to customer or client	Customer's or Client's

---

The Golden Rule of Introductions

"The Most Honored Person is Mentioned First."

Remember:

1. Status first
2. If equal status, then age, and then gender

Hugging at Work

In many cultures, hugging is not considered intimate, sexual, or seductive but is a genuine way to show friendship and warmth toward another person. Since the September 11, 2001, tragedies in the United States, more people have begun to hug each other in the workplace. Basically these hugs are not about intimacy but about giving comfort in troubling times.

Generally, as long as hugs are wanted and welcomed and not sexual in nature, they would not meet the definition of sexual harassment. However, before anyone gives a hug to anyone else in the workplace, he/she should ask permission. Even if the other person is crying or visibly upset, do not assume they need a hug. Ask if they would like one.

Exercise: Practicing Introductions

Directions: Introduce the following people (write out your scripts below):

1. Your supervisor to your spouse or significant other.

2. Yourself to the head of your organization.

3. A new coworker to your teammates.

Being Introduced

When introducing yourself, or when being introduced, always stand and extend your right hand. If the person is older or a higher-level executive, say, "I'm happy to meet you, Mr./Ms. Name," or "How do you do, Mr./Mrs. Name?" You may usually call younger people by their first names. If someone says "How do you do?" in response to your introduction, the proper response is, "How do you do?" or "Pleased to meet you." "How do you do?" is a greeting, and "Fine" is not the proper answer.

Remembering Names

1. Be sure you actually hear the other person's name.
2. Use their name as quickly as possible and often in conversation.
3. Make note of the person's prominent features as a means of associating their name with their features.
4. Find out more about the person to help remember them.
5. Concentrate on the person and the name you want to remember.
6. Visually write the person's name on his or her forehead.

When You Forget a Name

The best thing to do when you've been introduced to someone and you need to introduce them to someone else but you've forgotten their name is to be honest. Everyone occasionally forgets names; it's only human. If you do forget a name, don't panic! Simply admit your momentary lapse and say something like, "How could I possibly forget your name? I just heard it!" Or, "I'm sorry. Please tell me your name again."

When you meet someone who has forgotten your name, don't make them suffer. State your name at once. And if you want to greet someone who may not remember you, approach them by saying something like, "Hello, Kay. I'm Abbey Lane. We met at Dr. Howser's office several weeks ago." This assertive courtesy will take the pressure off the other person and establish an immediate rapport.

Clarifying Mispronounced Names

If the introduction you received was unclear, simply ask the individual to repeat it or say, "I didn't quite get your name." People like to have their name spoken correctly. They prefer that you ask for a clarification if you are in doubt.

If your name is mispronounced, you should kindly correct it one time. After that, you may have to endure answering to your mispronounced name.

Saying Good-Bye After the Introduction

Just before you walk away, it is always a good idea to say a word or two to someone you have just met. For example, say, "It was nice to meet you after all this time," or "I hope to see you again," or something similar. If you say, "I've heard so many things about you," be sure to add the word "good," as in "I've heard so many good things about you."

Small Talk

Without a little chitchat (trivial talk) we business people have no common ground for establishing rapport with each other. The social aspect of work often forces us to make small talk with people we hardly know. Don't worry about being clever or even original, however. Venture out with a statement about something you may have in common with the other person. Your primary purpose is to convey warmth and interest.

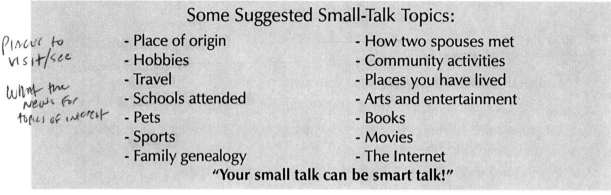

Some Suggested Small-Talk Topics:

- Place of origin	- How two spouses met
- Hobbies	- Community activities
- Travel	- Places you have lived
- Schools attended	- Arts and entertainment
- Pets	- Books
- Sports	- Movies
- Family genealogy	- The Internet

"Your small talk can be smart talk!"

Places to visit/see

What the news for topics of interest

Basic Guidelines for Small Talk

- Avoid using offensive language.
- Be kind in correcting another person.
- Use the word "you" more than "I."
- Ask open-ended questions.
- Feel confident that you have something to contribute to the conversation.
- Don't tell or laugh at ethnic jokes or off-color jokes.
- Don't interrupt.
- Don't correct another's grammar or pronunciation of words.
- Don't bear your soul.
- Don't bring up sensitive topics such as religion or politics.
- Don't be a complainer.
- Don't become known as a person who can only discuss work.
- Be prepared to share something about yourself.

Use small talk to learn about your colleagues—what drives them, what upsets them, what pleases them, what interest them. Don't squander small talk on yourself or your own needs and interests.

By effectively using casual, day-to-day small talk, you can:
- Establish and strengthen your position among your colleagues.
- Get leverage to secure support from your colleagues.
- Make the workplace experience more harmonious for everyone.

Effective communication at its best is called persuasion. Persuasion is based on the perception of gain. It is difficult to persuade someone to act in a certain way or to do something if that person feels either that he/she will not gain or profit from compliance or, even worse, will lose as a result of compliance. It is to your advantage to appeal to the self-interest of others. Small talk can help you learn about self-interest. The more you know about your colleagues, the more effectively you can communicate with them.

Exercise – Meeting and Greeting Quiz

Directions: Choose the most appropriate answer.

1. You are being introduced to a visitor. Unfortunately, you've been holding a cold drink and your hands are like ice. You:

    (A) Smile and greet the person, but keep your hand at your side for fear he or she will think you're cold.

    (B) Shake hands, but apologize for your hand, explaining that you've been holding a cold drink.

    (C) Blow into your palms before extending your hand.

2. Someone has just walked up to you and introduced herself, but you weren't listening very well and didn't get her name. You:

    (A) Don't ask again because you don't want to look stupid.

    (B) Ask again because you don't want to alienate a potential associate.

    (C) Go find somebody else so he can introduce himself to her and you can listen.

3. You are the assistant for the senior manager in your department. When your manager introduces you to a new coworker, you:

    (A) Smile, remain seated, and wait for the new coworker to extend his or her hand in deference to your position.

    (B) Stand up and offer your hand.

    (C) Get up quickly and hug the new coworker in an effort to make him or her feel welcome.

4. A female manager comes into a male manager's office. He should:

    (A) Rise and greet her.

    (B) Keep working at the computer.

    (C) Look up and greet her.

5. When introducing your supervisor to a visitor, you should first say:

    (A) The visitor's name.

    (B) Your supervisor's name.

    (C) Your name.

(Answers on page 93)

Exercise – Introducing Yourself

Directions: Role-play an introduction of yourself with another person and use small talk.

As you shake hands, take the opportunity to address the other person by name and repeat your own. Example: "Ms. Sutton, I'm (give first and last name) from (name department)." **Write your introduction first. Then list three possible small-talk topics.**

Accepting a Compliment with Grace

- A genuine compliment is a specific expression of appreciation given and received in a spirit of sincerity.
- It is important to say the right things when you accept a compliment and avoid saying and doing the wrong things.
- Accept a compliment by giving a compliment, not just thanks.
- Don't confess unworthiness.
- Don't respond with a long speech.
- When the compliment is from your supervisor:
  1. Start with "thank you." If you add something like, "Coming from you, that really means something," you have a perfectly adequate response.
  2. Consider using the occasion to build additional goodwill and good feeling between you and your boss. Begin by expressing your pleasure and gratitude. Express your regard for your boss, if appropriate.
  3. Share the praise with others who deserve it. Name names; recognize your colleagues and coworkers.
- Possible responses if your supervisor says:
  1. "You deserve it." Reply with: "I've had a good example set for me. You've given me a lot of support. It's meant a lot."
  2. "I don't give praise lightly." Reply with: "I know you don't. That's why I'm thrilled with your remarks. They mean a great deal to me."

Complimenting Someone

A compliment should be **sincere** and **specific**. You can follow the compliment with a question.

For example:

> "Those are lovely earrings—and so unique! Do they have a story?"
>
> "I've never seen eyeglass frames like that. Where did you find them?"
>
> "That's an interesting button on your lapel. What is its meaning?"

Chapter 4

BUSINESS DRESS AND GROOMING

BUSINESS DRESS AND GROOMING

It Matters*

Wardrobe, accessories, and grooming—each is an important part of the impression you create and how others view you. No other business skill is as visible as the way you package yourself. Image puts a frame around all your credentials.

Although time marches on and trends definitely influence our choices in business clothing, the following three things have not changed:

1. If you want the job, you have to look the part.
2. If you want the promotion, you have to look promotable.
3. If you want respect, you must dress as well as or better than your industry standards.

Appearance is one of the many tools that can be used to advance your career. You must first assess the environment in which you work or would like to work. Keep the following in mind:

- Dress in the uniform of the industry and the individual organization.

- Note that firms and businesses that are fiscal and traditional in orientation (for example, banks, insurance firms, legal and accounting firms, and government) are considered traditional so their dress codes are usually very conservative.

- Organizations that are sales- and marketing-oriented (for example, IT companies, advertising agencies, pharmaceutical companies, real estate firms, telephone and communications companies, and upscale automobile dealerships) may require employees to dress more contemporarily.

- Organizations that bridge both manual and office activity (engineering companies or departments, heavy manufacturing, and transportation) may require a more casual dress and/or uniforms.

- Creatively oriented businesses (for example retail, residential decorating, and cosmetics companies; publishing, design and music firms; and other creative businesses) are more trendy and may look for employees to dress in a sophisticated style.

- Business-Casual Days: The emphasis is still on business and not casual. It does not mean a tee shirt, jeans, shorts, cutoffs, tank tops or flip-flops. It means well-coordinated outfits.

When in doubt, dress conservatively.

---

* Chapter 10, "The Impact of a Business Wardrobe," page141, *Professional Presence* by Susan Bixler (Putnam Publishing Group: NY, 1991).

Some Grooming and Dressing No–No's

Clothing too tight and restrictive

Clothing too short

Clothing not pressed

Clothing soiled or dirty or torn

Dirty teeth

Bad breath

Dirty fingernails

Chipped fingernail polish

Extra-long fingernails

No socks or stockings (seasonal)

Dirty feet or toenails

Smelling of smoke

Heavy perfume or cologne

Heavy makeup

Distracting jewelry

T-shirts with messages

Chewing gum

Undergarments showing

Tight Spandex clothing

See-through clothing

Plunging necklines

Tank tops or halter tops

Dark hosiery with a white skirt

Ankle-high hosiery with a skirt

Blouses that reveal a bare midriff

Muscle shirts

Clothes that ride up

Safety pins showing

Men with poorly groomed facial hair

Toothpick in mouth

Slits in skirts that are more like slashes

Wearing unpolished shoes or shoes needing repair

Materials that are too dressy (taffeta) or too sheer

Exposed shoulders, backs, bosoms, midriffs, or thighs

Men in white socks and dress shoes

Slips of the wrong color showing through the slit

Unlined pants that reveal the wearer's underwear or lack thereof

Grooming Tips

- Nails for both men and women should be clean and fairly short with cuticles pushed back.
- Clear or subtly colored polish on nails that are 1/4 inch beyond the fingertip is the most attractive look.
- Makeup should be light and neutral.
- Hair should be shampooed regularly.
- Perfumes and fragrances should be subtle.
- Smelling clean is essential.

Ties

- Neckties make a strong impression. When in doubt, choose traditional patterns such as solids or stripes.
- Tie widths vary with changing fashion, but a safe rule of thumb is that the width of the tie should approximate the width of the suit lapels.
- The tied necktie should extend to the trouser belt but not below it.
- Tie the tie carefully and neatly.

The All-Important Windsor Knot

For men, one of the most important dressing skills is the ability to tie a Windsor knot. However, getting it right takes practice—hours of it—but the reward is a crisp, snappy-looking Windsor that will speak volumes about you.

The following diagram shows the eight-step method, and don't worry, even those experienced with the Windsor often need to start over because the wide end is too long or too short in relation to the narrow end.

Place tie around your neck with the wide end longer. Cross the wide end over the narrow end.

Bring the wide end up and through the noose. Pull it down tight.

Wrap the wide end back behind the knot and pull it out to your right.

Tuck the wide end into the noose and pull down on the left-hand side of the tie.

Bring the wide end across the front of the knot and pull to your right.

Bring the wide end up through the noose again.

Slip the wide end through the front of the knot and pull down.

Tighten it all up. If the lengths are not right, start over with wide and narrow lengths different.

Image puts a frame around all your credentials

Always Look Your Best

A tip for both men and women in the workplace: Keep a dark, long-sleeved jacket at work just in case you have to attend a meeting or have to meet VIPs and you are dressed casually. The jacket will give the appearance of a more formal look. Make sure you change it with the seasons.

Body Piercings and Tattoos

There is a current fashion, among younger people in particular, to pierce and/or tattoo just about every part of the body. General rule: Don't think about what you and your peers might like about your piercings or tattoos when they see them but rather focus on what others might think whenever they look at you. Do you want people to concentrate on your tattoo or eyebrow ring or on what you are saying? Note that in traditional-dress organizations, tattoos and piercings are frowned upon. Bottom line: unless you work at or own a tattoo parlor or piercing establishment or are in the entertainment business (i.e., with a rock or rap group), don't advertise your tattoos and/or body piercing on the job.

> **"The key is to present no visual surprises."**
> ~ June Hine Moore, *The Etiquette Advantage*

Exercise: Checking Out Your Role Model

Directions: Identify someone in top management whom you admire for their dress and grooming.

1. Describe how he or she dresses, including accessories (briefcase, pens, etc.). If it is a woman, how does she wear jewelry, her hair, and makeup? It is a man, how does he cut his hair/facial hair?

   Dress in pant / jacket - business casual
   small earrings, not lots of jewelry, or perfume, make up, minize, how put together

2. What messages do your role models convey about themselves through their appearance?

   Professional, All About business

3. What can you do to improve your dress and grooming based on what you have observed from your role models?

   Business casual - jean/Friday

Chapter 5

DINING ETIQUETTE

— 38 —

DINING ETIQUETTE

Table manners play an important part in making a favorable impression. Never underestimate the power of a meal, especially when it is in the context of conducting business. Your table manners can make a difference between getting that promotion or not, or between closing that business deal or not.

Napkins

1. Your napkin is the one on the left. Sometimes it is placed in a wine glass or serving plate directly in front of you.

2. Put your napkin in your lap as soon as you're seated or as soon as the host does it if you are a guest. Unfold the napkin halfway and place the fold toward your knees.

3. At a formal restaurant, the server will remove your napkin from the wine glass or serving plate and place it across your lap. You may tack the napkin into your belt (but not your collar) if you think it will help keep stains off your clothing.

4. If you need to leave the table, put your napkin on your chair when you leave, and put it back onto your lap when you return.

Reading the Table Setting

General Rule: Liquids will be on your right and solids will be on your left.

LEFT	RIGHT
~ Bread-and-Butter Plate	~ Glassware
~ Small Butter Knife	~ Cup and Saucer
(Placed horizontally across the	~ Knives
top of the bread plate)	~ Spoons
~ Salad Plate	~ Fish/Seafood Fork
~ Napkin (sometimes on the plate)	
~ Forks	

A Formal Setting

Ordering

1. It is better to find out before you order that a dish is prepared with something you do not like or are allergic to than to spend the entire meal picking tentatively at your food. If you have a question about how a dish is prepared, ask your server.

2. It is best to order foods that can be eaten with a knife and fork. Finger foods can be messy and are best left for informal dining.

3. As a guest, do not order one of the most expensive items on the menu or more than two courses unless your host indicates that it is alright.

4. If the host orders three courses, the guest should do the same. Otherwise, the pace of the meal will be ruined.

While Eating

1. Your food will be served from the left so expect the server to reach over your shoulder. Lean slightly right as this occurs.

2. Keep your elbows off the table while eating, but you may rest your forearms there between courses.

3. As you eat, use your silverware from the outside in.

4. Bring food to your mouth, not your mouth to your food.

5. If you need to leave the table in the middle of a course or if you pause eating, place your folk and knife on your plate in an inverted V, with the fork tines face down. This is a signal to the server that you're not finished.

6. If food spills off your plate, you may pick it up with a piece of your silverware and place it on the edge of your plate.

7. If you need to send something back to the kitchen, don't make a big deal or it, and don't announce it to the rest of the table.

8. Never spit a piece of bad food or tough gristle into your napkin. Remove the food from your mouth using the same utensil it went in with. Place the piece of food on the edge of your plate. If possible, cover it with some other food from your plate.

9. A used piece of silverware should never be put on the table.

10. Excuse yourself for all biological functions, including the need to blow your nose. Blowing your nose on the restaurant's napkins—paper or otherwise—is bad form. So is using a toothpick at the table.

11. It is inappropriate to ask for a doggy bag when you are a guest. Save the doggy bag for informal dining situations.

Sorbet or Intermezzo

A sorbet or intermezzo (favored water ice) may be served between the appetizer and the entree to cleanse the palate. You need to have only a small taste. It is not necessary to finish the entire dish.

Helpful Dining Tips

1. Scoop your soup away from you.

2. Use your knife and fork to cut larger, flat pasta such as lasagna; use your knife and spoon to swirl long, string pasta such as spaghetti.

3. If you have a shrimp cocktail, use your cocktail fork to bring the pieces to your mouth.

4. Use your knife to cut fruit from the core and your fork to bring the pieces to your mouth.

5. When eating shellfish, hold the shell with your hand and eat the meat with a cocktail fork. Do not stack the shells.

6. When eating steak, cut and eat one piece at a time.

7. Use your knife and fork with lamb or pork chops.

8. Use your knife to push food onto the fork or use your fork to spear your food.

9. Cut off the tail and head of a whole fish, cut along the backbone, fold the meat back, remove the whole skeleton, and set it aside before you begin eating. You may ask the server to do this for you.

10. Vegetables served in side dishes can be eaten out of the dish or placed onto your plate.

11. Never leave your spoon in a cup after using it. Put it on the saucer.

12. To eat raw, uncut strawberries, hold them by the hull.

13. Raw apple pieces may be eaten with your fingers.

14. At a clam bar, it's acceptable to suck the clam off the shell. At a restaurant, use a fork for the clam, a spoon for the broth.

15. You may spread cheese with either a fork or a knife.

16. You may sip your coffee or tea with a spoon when it's too hot to drink normally.

17. Eat limp bacon with a fork, crisp bacon with your fingers.

18. You may eat the green "fat" from a lobster.

19. Fruit pits should go untouched from mouth to spoon to edge of plate.

20. After using sugar out of a packet or butter off a paper square, put the paper under the edge of your butter plate.

21. Use a spoon to get jam out of a jar, then rest it on your butter plate. Use your knife to get the jam to your bread.

22. Eat artichoke leaves with your fingers.

23. You may eat firm asparagus with your fingers at an informal dinner.

24. It is not necessary to cut olives or cherry tomatoes before eating.

25. You may drink your soup if it is served in a cup with handles.

26. Wine glasses for white wine and champagne are held by the stem; red wine and brandy glasses are held by the bowl.

27. Salads may be served before or after the main course.

28. When bread is served half-sliced in a basket with a napkin, take a portion of the napkin in your left hand and hold a piece of the bread, then use your right hand to tear off a piece.

29. Never use the knife on the butter dish to butter your bread.

30. A clear soup is served with a large, oval soup spoon (know as a bouillon spoon). A cream soup is served with a small, round soup spoon.

31. If you are at a casual dining function, you can eat fried chicken with your hands. If it's a more formal occasion, cut the meat from the bones with your knife and fork.

32. All food should be eaten in manageable bites without overfilling the mouth.

33. Close your mouth when you eat and never talk with a mouth full of food.

34. Pass both the salt and the pepper when asked for either one.

35. Always say, "Please pass the ..."

36. Refuse a beverage by simply saying, "No, thank you." Do not invert the cup or glass.

37. Modify the volume of your voice so only the people at the dining table can hear you.

38. Never leave your purse, keys, sunglasses, or eyeglasses on the table.

Holding Eating Utensils

1. Both spoon and fork should be held horizontally by balancing them between the first knuckle of the middle finger and the tip of the index finger while steadying the handle with your thumb.

2. The knife should be used with the tip of the index finger gently pressing out over the top of the blade to guide as you cut.

3. Hold your spoon like a pencil, with the handle between your index finger and middle finger and your thumb on top. Dip the spoon away from you in a horizontal position.

4. Never grab your fork and hold it as if it were a shovel.

5. Never hold your knife and fork vertically.

6. Keep your elbows from flapping; hold them close to the body.

7. If you realize you've picked up the wrong utensil, don't put it down and start again. Just continue to eat.

Soup Spoon Usage

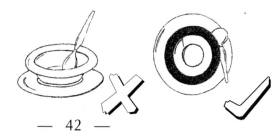

Finger Bowls

A finger bowl is presented after the main course and before dessert arrives. Your server places it in front of you on a plate, usually with a doily under the bowl. The bowl contains warm water with a slice of lemon and occasionally a small flower. A small dessert fork and spoon are also on the plate. Move these utensils down and place them to the left and right, respectively, of where the dessert plate will go.

Passing Food

1. When you need to pass items around the table, always pass them to your guests first, usually counterclockwise.

2. If you are asked to pass the bread or rolls, pass the butter too without being asked.

3. When the butter comes to you, place a small amount on your bread plate. If you do not have a bread plate, put some butter on the edge of your dinner plate. Break your bread into small pieces and butter it one bite at a time, keeping the pieces on your bread plate or on the table next to your forks.

4. If your server places coffee or tea on the table without pouring it, the person closest to the pot should offer to pour.

5. You may reach for anything within easy reach, but do not reach across the table.

When You Have Finished

1. Never push your plate toward the center of the table when you are finished.

2. Once the meal is over, place your napkin neatly on the table to the right of your dinner plate. Do not refold your napkin, but don't wad it up either.

3. Put your silverware in the finished position to signal that you have completed the meal. Imagine your plate is the face of a clock. Place the knife in the 10 and 4 position with the cutting edge facing the center of the plate. The tip of the knife should point to 10 and the handle to 4. Place the fork, tine down, parallel to and just below the knife. The handles will extend toward the lower right-hand side of the plate.

The rest position tells your server that you're still eating

The finished position tells your server that you've finished

FYI: The custom of serving the salad before the entree (main course) originated in California to appease hungry, impatient diners. In other parts of the world, the salad is served after the main course and before dessert.

Helpful Dining Illustrations

Glassware

From left:
A. White wine goblet
B. Champagne flute
C. Champagne coupe
D. Sherry glass
E. Cordial glass
F. Brandy snifter
G. Cocktail glass
H. Old-fashioned glass
I. Pilsner glass

The Six Forks

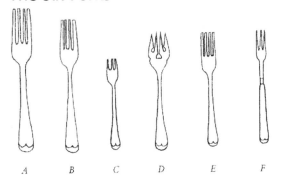

From left:
A. Dinner fork
B. Salad fork
C. Oyster fork
D. Fish fork
E. Dessert fork
F. Fruit fork

The Seven Spoons

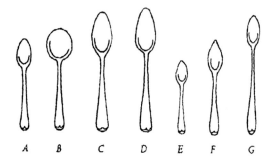

From left:
A. Teaspoon
B. Round soup spoon
C. Oval soup spoon
D. Dessert spoon
E. Demitasse spoon
F. Grapefruit spoon
G. Iced-tea spoon

The Six Knives
(Though there are six knives, you are most likely to encounter only three or four.)

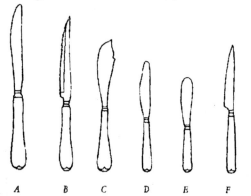

From left:
A. Dinner knife
B. Steak knife
C. Fish knife
D. Butter knife
E. Butter spreader
F. Fruit knife

Dining No–No's

1. Don't talk on your cell phone at the table. If you absolutely must make a call, go to a private spot.
2. Don't put your napkin around your neck. Keep it in your lap.
3. Don't season your food before tasting it.
4. Avoid blotting lipstick on linen napkins. Don't pat your lips, wipe around them.
5. Don't saw your roll in half and make a butter sandwich.
6. Don't let the server become part of the meal. Never engage in excessive banter that detracts from the table conversation.
7. Don't apply makeup, not even lipstick, at the table.
8. Don't put your handbag on the table.
9. Don't smoke during a meal, even if you sitting in the smoking section.

The Business Lunch

- Lunch is the most popular business meal.
- Avoid the lunch crunch—don't waste time fighting crowds.
- Schedule your lunch early or at a restaurant that takes lunch reservations.
- Don't talk business until after everyone has looked at the menu and ordered.
- Don't drink hard liquor at lunch—it creates the impression that you have a drinking problem.
- If you must drink an alcoholic beverage, limit yourself to one glass of wine or beer.

Exercise – Dining Etiquette Quiz

Directions: Circle either T for True or F for False

T	F	1.	If you are asked to pass the bread or rolls, always pass the butter too without being asked.
T	F	2.	Scoop your soup away from you.
T	F	3.	Your food will be served from the right so expect the server to reach over your shoulder.
T	F	4.	As you eat, use your silverware from the inside out.
T	F	5.	It is okay to apply makeup, even lipstick, at the dining table.
T	F	6.	A used piece of silverware should never be put on the table.
T	F	7.	The general rule of table setting is "liquids on your right and solids on your left."
T	F	8.	Your napkin is the one on the left.
T	F	9.	If your server places coffee or tea on the dining table without pouring, the person closest to the pot should offer to pour.
T	F	10.	Never push your plate toward the center of the table when you are finished.
T	F	11.	Never leave your spoon in the cup after using it. Put it on the saucer.
T	F	12.	Don't put your napkin in your lap as soon as you're seated.
T	F	13.	Bring your food to your mouth and not your mouth to your food.
T	F	14.	Don't put your handbag on the table.
T	F	15.	It is not necessary to cut olives or cherry tomatoes before eating.
T	F	16.	Dinner is the most popular business meal.
T	F	17.	If you must drink an alcoholic beverage at lunch, limit yourself to one glass of wine or beer.
T	F	18.	The placement of your eating utensils informs your server that you are finished.
T	F	19.	Forks are placed to the left of the plate, and knives and spoons to the right.
T	F	20.	The finger bowl is presented after the main course and before dessert arrives.

(Answers on page 93)

Chapter 6

NONVERBAL COMMUNICATION

NONVERBAL COMMUNICATION

Body Language

Body language can more accurately be described as nonverbal communication since it involves more than just our bodies. Nonverbal communication includes factors such as use of time and space, distance between persons when conversing, use of color, dress, walking behavior, standing, positioning, seating arrangement, office locations, and furnishings. The number of things that can be taken into consideration as far as nonverbal communication is concerned is almost endless.

It is important for you to understand how you communicate nonverbally. Why? Your nonverbal communication often speaks louder than your words, even though such communication is so subtle that most of the time people are not even aware they are doing it. Of the total impact of a message, 7% is verbal (word choice), 38% is vocal (oral presentation), and 58% is body language.

Nonverbal communication conveys messages that are more believable than verbal language. If overdone or underdone, your body language can backfire and create a negative impression that is not always easy to overcome. What does your body language say about you?

Nonverbal communication is an art form and not an exact science. There is no mathematical formula that can give you professional presence; however, there are some concepts that apply. Some of the primary aspects of body language are eye contact, facial expressions, body posture and moment, hand gestures, touching, and physical distance. Before discussing these aspects, we need to examine what people are looking for—that is, how people perceive others.

Dr. Janet Elsea's Nine Factors

People, like books, are often judged by their covers. Dr. Janet Elsea, in her book, *First Impressions, Best Impressions*, lists nine factors that people notice when meeting each other, ranked in order of importance. We have no control over the first three factors. At least six factors are related to communication. All have implications for the impression we make on others, and ultimately on our opportunities to get hired or to advance in an organization.

1 – Skin Color; 2 – Gender; 3 – Age; 4 – Appearance; 5 – Facial Expressions; 6 – Eye Contact; 7 – Movement; 8 – Personal Space; 9 – Touch.

Looking for Cues

According to psychologist Dr. Egon Brunswick, what we think we see in others influences how we treat and respond to them. When Person A talks with Person B, both go through the process of adaptation or coming to terms with each other. This adaptation is necessary to enhance the quality of the relationship they develop. Some call this "reading people."

The adaptation process is conducted through our personal lenses (like eyeglass lenses), which are always present. Our lenses have perceptual filters that can cloud and distort an image. Our filters are affected by factors such as race, age, gender, sexual orientation, and so forth.

To compensate for these filters and make an adaptation, we establish traits. These traits can be defined as characteristics or attributes we see in ourselves or as values we want to see in the people we interact with and are willing to trust. We want people to have the same traits as we do; however, these traits, which are inaccessible to the naked eye, are not necessarily easy to define (i.e., honesty, loyalty, friendliness, etc.). Yet we want and need them in order to form judgments about others. What people do is to look for more observable and tangible cues (signals or signs), which they believe stand for the central trait they are interested in but cannot see.

People establish or identify cues to associate with their desired traits. For example, one may equate honesty with direct eye contact. Sales representatives, scam artists, and thieves, however, have been taught the value of this cue and use it opportunistically. Unfortunately, according to Dr. Brunswick, our cues are only 50% accurate. A constant reliance on the same cues to view all people in particular categories such as race, gender, or regionality results in stereotyping. Therefore, the more you know about others, the more you can tailor your nonverbal cues to meet their expectations.

Nonverbal communication is a primary cue that people use to evaluate you. No matter if the cue is accurate or not, people will look for it to establish your traits.

> Nonverbal communication—from appearance to facial expressions to movement—is the primary ingredient in the recipe people use to judge what is "attractive" in others.

EXERCISE: Identifying Cues

1. Identify the cues used by your manager and/or supervisor at work.

2. Identify the cues you use at work.

3. What are the similarities and differences between your cues and those of your manager and/or supervisor?

Some of the primary aspects of body language are **eye contact, facial expressions, body posture and movement, hand gestures, touching, physical distance (space),** and **appearance.** Knowledge and application of the following information can enhance your professional image.

Eye Contact

- The eye area is one of the least controllable regions of your face and, as a result, your eyes can reveal much about your emotional state. There is a significant change in your eyes when you are surprised or fearful but little change when you feel happiness or disgust. In U.S. culture, direct eye contact with a speaker indicates interest and attention.

- A rule of thumb for effective eye contact is to make it direct, but adjust it according to comfort level. In normal conversation, each eye contact lasts only about a second before one or both individuals look away. Without eye contact, however, you could be perceived as submissive, nervous, or untruthful.

- If you have a problem making direct eye contact, focus instead on the speaker's nose, ears, or forehead. The speaker will still think you are making eye contact.

- To effectively use eye contact and avoid offending or alienating others, you must take into account cultural differences. Some Americans of Asian descent and some American Indians, for example, might find direct eye contact unsettling, even threatening, or as a sign of disrespect or hostility. For them, making direct eye contact with another may be difficult or discomforting.

Facial Expressions

- Facial expressions are the cues most people rely on most often in initial interactions. After your overall appearance, your face is the most visible part of you, by which others read your mood and personality.

- Happiness is shown in the cheeks/mouth and eye/eyelid areas. Sadness and fear are conveyed in the eye/eyelid areas. Surprise is conveyed in the cheek/mouth, eye/eyelid, and brow/forehead areas. Anger is most evident in the lower face (mouth) and brow/forehead areas.

- Know what your facial expressions communicate. Remember, they are the main cues that others rely on most to gauge your attitude, feelings, and emotional state. You might be able to "fool" yourself into feeling better than you really do simply by smiling, but you cannot fool others.

- Don't interpret a facial expression entirely from your own point of view. The face is more easily controlled than other parts of the body. It can often be an unreliable source of information about what's going on inside its owner's mind.

- The facial expressions you wear are influenced by your socioeconomic level, cultural background, gender, ethnicity, gender, and age. Consider the following:
  - High-status people smile less than low-status people.
  - Women smile more than men, often in direct contradiction to the message they are conveying.

- Make sure your facial expression sets a positive tone before you even begin to speak.

Body Posture and Movement

- Good posture makes you look taller and more in command, and it is essential for proper voice control.

- Keep your body straight but not rigid. Your shoulders should be even and both feet on the ground (not planted, but weight evenly distributed). This position, whether sitting or standing, gives you flexibility to move or lean forward (both signs of interest and listening) or to lean or move back (suggesting disagreement, annoyance, boredom, or relaxation).

- Movement is a critical aspect in the presentation of a confident, assured impression. Walk and posture are closely tied to emotional state. A wealth of information is available merely in how someone moves. A person's level of confidence, degree of anxiety, and efforts to deceive are evident to those who know how to "read" body movements.

- If you are more interested in the emotional state of another person, observe them from the neck down. This part of the body reveals much information. Look for:
  - Jerky, disjointed movements as a sign that the person is nervous or in conflict;
  - Slumped posture and shuffling movements as signals of depression or alienation; and
  - Rushed walk or gestures as indicators of stress and anxiety.

- Walk briskly (not too fast or too slowly), stand and sit "tall," and you will look and feel more confident. Your voice will confirm this by sounding strong and resonant.

- When you rise to meet someone who is entering your cubicle or office, you indicate that you are taking the opporunity to talk with them seriously. If you just lodge back in your chair, you might signal that you are disinterested or that the standing person can control the conversation.

- Slide into a seat, don't flop into it. Keep your feet on the floor, knees facing forward or to the side. You may cross your legs or cross them at the ankle. If you are a woman wearing a skirt, you may cross one knee over the other. Most people look uncoordinated if they let their legs just dangle awkwardly.

- In the U.S., men typically nod to symbolize that they agree. Women typically nod just to express that they are taking in information.

- Tilting one's head to the side indicates interest and close listening.

- During a meal, keep both feet flat on the floor or cross your feet at the ankles. Don't cross your legs at the knee, and don't prop your feet on the chair or table legs or wrap them around anything handy under the table.

- As you eat, sit straight on the front three-quarters of your chair.

Hand Gestures

- Next to the head and face, the hands are the most fluent conveyors of body language. In the U.S., open hands, palms up, suggest honesty and openness. Rubbing the hands together communicates positive energy. Putting your fingers together in steeple-fashion conveys confidence.

- In nearly all cultures, people want to see your hands and wonder what's going on with them when they can't. It's best to hold your hands where they can be seen and where you can gesture naturally, to illustrate what you're saying or to regulate a conversation.

- When using your hands while talking, avoid wiping your nose, touching your face, or scratching "private" parts of your body. Don't fiddle with coins, bracelets, keys, pens, ties, or other objects.

- Hand gestures are most effective when they emphasize the content and importance of what you say. Gesture with purpose and always face toward your viewer.

- Gestures should be natural movements and should not distract from your conversation. Don't make big, unnatural, exaggerated, or distracting movements.

- One caution about gestures: Realize that a friendly gesture used in the U.S. could be an obscene gesture in another culture.

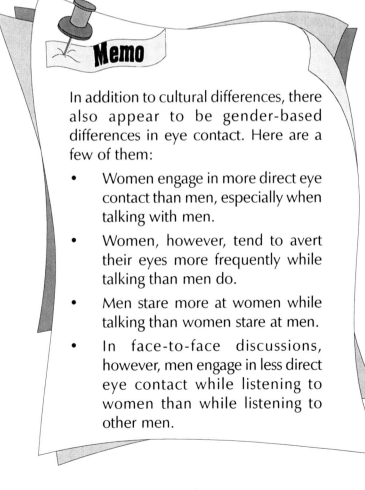

Memo

In addition to cultural differences, there also appear to be gender-based differences in eye contact. Here are a few of them:

- Women engage in more direct eye contact than men, especially when talking with men.

- Women, however, tend to avert their eyes more frequently while talking than men do.

- Men stare more at women while talking than women stare at men.

- In face-to-face discussions, however, men engage in less direct eye contact while listening to women than while listening to other men.

Touching

- Touching is the only aspect of nonverbal communication that involves physical contact with another person. Touching can be a powerful means of expression. Physical contact, regardless of cultural background, is important for healthy human development.

- Touching differs from culture to culture. Relative to other cultures, the U.S. is a non-contact culture.

- Touching means different things to different people. Touching may express:
  - A power relationship—typically the person with more power is permitted to touch those with less power.
  - A greeting—handshaking, embracing, and kissing may be considered intimate in some cultures, but not in others.
  - A way to gain attention or acceptance—a pat on the arm or shoulder.
  - A way to congratulate or encourage someone—handshake or embrace.
  - Rage or anger—aggressive touching or patting is totally inappropriate in any setting.
  - A way to gain favor—touching someone when asking for a favor is acceptable in some cultures.
  - The desire for a close relationship—affectionate, seductive, or sexual touches are often disguised and used in improper settings.

- In the U.S., except in a few well-defined situations (i.e., shaking hands), touching is generally associated with intimate, interpersonal relationships. The best advice is to avoid touching another person in a business setting unless that person invites the touch.

EXERCISE — Touching at Work

Think of the people you interact with at work, especially those who are of a different gender, race, or cultural background, and ask yourself the following questions:

1. Whom do I touch?
   - What does it mean to me?
   - Is it welcomed?
   - What does it mean to the other person?
   - How do they react?
   - Do they touch back?

2. Who touches me?
   - What does it mean to me?
   - Is it alright with me?
   - What does it mean to them?

3. If the other person's touching is unwelcomed, have I made it known to them that their touches are uncomfortable or not acceptable?
   - If not, how could I tell them this?

Physical Distance (Space)

- In his book, *The Silent Language*, Edward T. Hall points out that people have several kinds of space surrounding them:

  1. Intimate Space—This distance extends from contact to about 18 inches out. This distance encourages soft whispers about very confidential matters. It also allows people to use more of their senses in communicating (for example, touching and smelling).

  2. Personal Space—This distance ranges from 18 inches to about 4 feet away from a person. Conversation is usually soft and topics are usually personal.

  3. Social Space—This distance refers to a separating distance of between 4 to 12 feet. At this distance, voices are usually raised and the topics are nonpersonal public information for anyone to hear.

  4. Public Space—This is any distance beyond social space, from 12 feet and beyond. A loud voice must be used and impersonal topics are discussed at this distance.

- How much space a person needs will depend on his or her background, gender, age, and culture. However, in the work environment, social space distance seems most appropriate.

- Recognize that others may have different views about space than you do. When you first encounter people and begin talking with them, don't move—allow the other person to adjust to their comfort level. Pay attention to how you feel if the distance they select seems "uncomfortable" to you. If you want to become more informal, close the space between you very slowly. As you move, be attentive to the other person's reactions for an indication that you are getting "too close."

- Your personal "bubble of privacy" or "comfort zone" depends on:
  - Your size, height, and weight
  - Your cultural background
  - Whom you are with and how well you like each other
  - How much power and authority is being wielded and by whom
  - Whether you are male or female.

- You expand or contract your personal space according to how intimate you want an encounter with another person to be. Here are some examples of the effect that power, gender, and culture have on the size of one's territory, as well as some ways people defend their own space or invade someone else's:
  - High-status people are given more space in nearly all cultures than are low-status people.
  - High-status people tend to "own," and are granted, more desirable spatial positions (the proverbial "corner office," for example).
  - Aggressive people tend to take up, and are granted, more space than do less dominant people.
  - Men generally occupy more personal space than women.
  - Women's space tends to be violated by others more often than does men's space.

Appearance

- Appearance includes much more than just dress or clothing. It also takes into account the following:
    - Facial attractiveness
    - Body type (size, weight, height)
    - Posture (sitting and standing)
    - Hair style (or lack of hair) and facial hair (beard, moustache, or goatee)
    - Accessories (purses, shoes, jewelry, tie clasps, glasses, briefcase, pens, notebooks, and so on)
    - Smells (perfumes, aftershaves, body odors)
    - Color (skin, clothing, makeup).
- It is important to understand the effect appearance has on you and others.
- Dress for the job, client, or organization you have targeted, not the one you presently have. You may need to dress more formally or informally depending on the setting.
- Spend money on a professional-looking wardrobe. You feel better about yourself when you feel you look good.

Exercise: Assessing Your Appearance

Answer the following questions

1. What is the dress code within your organization? Is there a dress code?

2. What are employees expected to wear? What should employees never wear?

3. What feedback, good or bad, have you gotten on your appearance at work?

4. If you need to improve, what steps can you take to improve your professional image?

Nonverbal Communication and Making an Entrance

Nonverbal communication begins before you utter a single word. Therefore, how you enter a room makes a powerful statement about who you think you are and how others will perceive you. Below are some general guidelines to help you sharpen your nonverbal communication when making an entrance:

1. **Walk Tall and Enter with a Communication Goal**
   - Practice walking tall. Never enter a room or approach another person in a cringing, stooped, or slouched manner. Concentrate on maintaining an erect posture as you make your entrance.
   - Know your communication goal before you enter. Do not appear hesitant or absent-minded.

2. **Smile**
   - A genuine smile, not an artificial one, will put people at ease. If you appear cold or hard, some people you approach will decide that you are unapproachable or not worth the effort to interact with.
   - Smile as you enter a room, and you can fool yourself into feeling more confident.

3. **Make Eye Contact**
   - To exploit the sparkle in your eyes, to convey openness and transmit energy, make eye contact immediately, before the first words are spoken.
   - If you have a problem making direct eye contact, focus on the speaker's nose, ears, or forehead. It gives the appearance of direct eye contact.

4. **Give a Professional Handshake**
   - People remember touch—contact—as much as they do words. Your handshake should convey confidence, openness, straightforward warmth, and a willingness to communicate.

5. **Think Before You Sit**
   - Don't rush to take a seat; doing so will make you appear anxious.
   - Always choose a firm chair rather than a sofa or a very soft chair. You want a chair that keeps you upright and allows you to maintain an erect posture.
   - Unless you are running a meeting, do not sit at the head of the conference table. The person with the highest position should sit at the head of the table.

6. **Convey Relaxed Energy**
   - Poise begins with breathing. When you become upset, nervous, or scared, breathing typically becomes shallower, shorter, and faster. Control your breathing to keep from communicating nervousness.

7. **Use Your Head, Face, and Hands**
   - Your head, face, and hands convey a lot of body language. Make sure they all convey the same message.

8. **Learn to Use Your Voice**
   - Deep voices are generally perceived as more persuasive than high-pitched ones. This is true for women as well as men.
   - If your voice is pitched in the higher registers, consider consciously speaking in a lower pitch. Pitching your voice lower has the benefit of producing a more pleasing tone. It also has the effect of slowing you down, thereby encouraging more precise articulation of your words.

9. **Communicate a Professional Presence with Clothing and Good Grooming**
   - Know the appropriate dress code for your organization.

EXERCISE – Nonverbal Feedback

Nonverbal feedback is being expressed all the time, all around you. Though no expression or gesture has one universal meaning, over your lifetime you have acquired a vocabulary of nonverbal expressions just as you have amassed a vocabulary of words. Try this exercise out with a friend: Just using facial expressions and posture, try to communicate the following attitudes:

1. Openness to what a speaker is saying
2. Lack of interest
3. Interest
4. Unwillingness to listen
5. Disagreement
6. Agreement
7. Worry
8. Boredom
9. Thoughtfulness
10. Excitement

Read the following descriptions of postures, facial expressions, and actions. Write down what you think each one is likely to communicate to another person:

1. Leaning forward in a chair

2. Leaning back in a chair, arms folded

3. Resting one's chin in both hands

4. Yawning

5. Smiling

6. Frowning

7. Smiling and nodding

8. Glancing at one's watch

9. Looking around the room

10. Tapping your fingers on a table

(Answers on page 93)

Chapter 7

Verbal Communication

VERBAL COMMUNICATION

Exercise: Listening to the Sound of Your Own Voice

Directions: Below are different voice styles by which people communicate. Which seem to best describe yours? Circle the numbers for the one(s) with which you identify most:

1.   My voice becomes agitated and/or loud when I am angry.

2.   I speak more quickly when nervous.

3.   I shout when I am passionate about the topic.

4.   I whisper when I am nervous.

5.   My voice slows significantly and/or becomes quieter when I get tired.

6.   Others describe my tone of voice as pleasant.

7.   Friends regard my tone of voice in a serious conversation as warm and understanding.

8.   I can control my tone of voice in most situations.

9.   I can control my volume in most situations.

10.   My voice can sound authoritarian and demanding when required.

11.   Others consider my voice meek.

12.   I'm lucky because my voice is clear, direct, and natural.

13.   My vocabulary and style of speaking tend to be serious and scholarly.

14.   My vocabulary and style of speaking tend to be common and abrupt.

If you checked any or all of the following, you need to work on your voice:
1, 2, 3, 4, 5, 10, 11, 14.

Your Best Voice

We all have voices that sound different. Some of us have the deep voice of authority, while others of us sound meek or frail. Voices can be pleasant or annoying, easy to decipher or unintelligible, clear as a bell or squeaky. The voice you project is determined by four factors, all of which can be controlled:

- *Energy*—The energy in your voice reflects a positive attitude and enthusiasm.

- *Rate of Speech*—A normal rate of speech is 125 – 175 words per minute. Speaking faster can create comprehension problems.

- *Pitch and Tone*—This can be a monotone, low, or high pitch. Ideally, you should vary your tone and inflection.

- *Quality*—All the above factors make up your voice quality.

There are several things you can do to produce a more desirable speaking voice. Some of these include:

1. Warm up by humming a song. This will help deepen the pitch and tone of your voice.

2. Practice your pitch and tone control by calling your telephone answering machine and recording several messages, then listen to the playback and critique yourself or ask a friend for help.

3. Role play with a friend and tape-record the conversation. Review it for tone, rate of delivery, etc.

4. Take a speech class at a local college or extension program to learn some voice exercises to help you avoid sounding monotonous.

5. PUT A SMILE INTO YOUR VOICE. It's easy to do. Simply remember to smile as you answer a call. Believe it or not, your voice will sound friendlier.

Notes:
§ ARTICULATION—How clearly are you speaking?

§ PITCH—What is the relative highness or lowness of your voice?

§ PACE—At what rate of speed do you speak?

§ TONE—What emotions are reflected in your voice?

Polishing Your Speaking Habits

Your voice can be an asset or a liability. To cultivate a pleasant voice:

- *Relax.* If you are tense, it will be reflected in your voice. Keep it well modulated; speak slowly and distinctly. It is amazing how much influence speaking quietly can have when someone else is rushed or irritated. Before you start talking, take a few deep breaths, relax your jaw muscles, and feel the tension lessen.

- *Read aloud.* If you have no one to read to, read to yourself. Practice varying your pitch. Read the same paragraph over several times and express a different emotion for each reading (i.e., happiness, excitement, fear, hostility, sympathy).

- *Control your volume.* Try to speak forcefully without screaming and softly without sounding uninteresting.

- *Separate your words.* If you speak too quickly, you may run one word into the next. Make your conversation easier to understand by speaking slowly and deliberately.

- *Enunciate distinctly.* Pronounce vowels clearly. Pay particular attention to word endings.

- *Pronounce each syllable.* Many words are mispronounced (or sound as though they are) because speakers slur over, omit, or add syllables. Speak with precision.

- *Smile.* Read a paragraph while you are smiling; reread the same words with a deep frown on your face. Notice the difference? If you want your voice to sound warm and friendly, smile while you are speaking. A frown can be heard.

- *Be enthusiastic.* Keep your voice animated and interesting. You can't expect people to accept ideas you offer in a low unemotional tone.

Remember that good speech will always be a great asset to you. It is the mark of a cultivated person. Take pride in your voice and your speaking manner.

Silence

The appropriate use of silence is an important communication skill to master. Yet, because we live in such a stimulus-filled world, silence is both unfamiliar and uncomfortable. When we rush in with chatter to fill the void, we can lose control of the communication encounter. When we talk too much, we eventually give away too much information. The most powerful use of silence is in focused listening, neither thinking about what you are going to say next nor scheming about how to convince another person. Focused listening means mental concentration and physical alertness. Giving a speaker your undivided attention, acknowledging that person with nods and other nonverbal encouragement, being patient and not interrupting creates an atmosphere of trust. The better listener in any encounter will end up with more information, and information is power. Taking notes is a silent form of flattery in the business world. Writing what someone has said into a permanent record shows your respect.

Speech Exercises

The following exercises are best done with someone who can give you feedback.

Articulation Exercise

Directions: Repeat aloud the following sentences until you can do so clearly:

1. Let's push cushions with much lush plush.
2. The whispering watchman waited while the woman whined.
3. The apt planner wrapped paper around the heap of typed papers.

Tone Exercise

Directions: Read the sentences below aloud: (1) with a smile, (2) with a look of happy surprise, (3) with a look of shock, and (4) with a frown on your face.

SMILE	"What are you doing here?"
HAPPY SURPRISE	"What are you doing here?"
SHOCK	"What are you doing here?"
FROWN	"What are you doing here?"

Pitch Exercise

Directions: Read the following sentences and put emphasis on the words in bold:

- Why haven't I **seen** you lately?
- Why haven't I seen you **lately**?
- Why **haven't I seen you** lately?

Pace Exercise

Directions:

1. Start speaking at your normal rate.
2. **Speed up** where words are *italicized*.
3. **Slow down** where words are underlined.

One evening John decided to go to his office to clear up some work. *It was a rainy night, and he had nothing better to do.* So he got into his car and drove to the city. As he approached his building, he noticed that there was a light on in his office and that his office window was open. While he watched, he saw two masked men going through his desk. John spun his car around and raced to the police station.

Communicating with People Who Speak English as a Second Language

When English is a person's second language and he/she is translating from one language to another, the person must:

1. Hear the words in English.
2. Think about it in their native language.
3. Arrive at a response in their native language.
4. Translate the answer into English in their mind.
5. Provide the response in English.

This why some non-native English speakers respond a little more slowly when talking in English.

Some guidelines when communicating with non-native English speakers:

1. Don't pretend to understand if you don't.
   - Ask the person to slow down. Say, "Excuse me. I am having a little trouble understanding you. Please slow down and repeat what you said so I can understand."

2. Ask questions when in doubt.
   - Ask open-ended questions that start with How, What, When, Where, or Why that cannot be answered with a Yes or No response.
   - Ask closed questions that can be answered with a simple Yes or No.

3. Don't rush the person.
   - Encourage the person to take his/her time.

4. Don't shout.
   - Speak clearly without raising your voice.
   - Remember that they are not hard of hearing.

5. Don't be rude.
   - Be polite and helpful.
   - Remember it is up to you to be helpful.

EXERCISE – Polishing Your Speaking Habits

Below are a few practice drills. Tape-record your voice reading the drills, then listen to your voice as you read.

All the Speech Sounds of the English Language

An old lighthouse keeper found an old map which he studied carefully and was able to decipher. From the peculiar lines and signs, he was able to make it out after a careful study. The directions were to dig four feet from the lighthouse and five feet underground for a rare chest of treasure. So, with a new pick and shovel, he was sure he could follow the instructions exactly. However, after several tries he dug through the earth and began lifting out the box of treasure. Suddenly he fell back as the treasure disintegrated into a thousand pieces and became nothing. That night he slept a wiser man.

Tongue Tripper Test Used for Applicants for TV-Radio Jobs

I bought a batch of baking powder and baked a batch of biscuits. I bought a big basket of biscuits back to the bakery and baked a basket of big biscuits. Then I took a big basket of biscuits and the basket of big biscuits and mixed the big biscuits with the basket of biscuits that was next to the big basket and a put a bunch of biscuits from the basket into a box. The I took the box of mixed biscuits and a biscuit mixer and a biscuit basket and bought the basket of biscuits and the box of mixed biscuits and the biscuit mixer to the bakery and opened a can of sardines.

For People with Closed Mouths

Sarah Shuster said Susie Simpson, Sam Simpson's sister, shouted she saw seven short shivering soldiers sadly standing on the shining, sandy seashore, severely shaking six sick, shy, shorn sheep sold by the sheriff for sixty cents.

For People with Lazy Lips

Betty Botter bought a bit of butter. "But," she said, "This butter's bitter. If I put it in my batter, it will make my batter bitter. But a bit of better butter will make my batter better." So Betty Botter bought a bit of better butter and made her batter better.

Chapter 8

ELECTRONIC COMMUNICATION

ELECTRONIC COMMUNICATION

Telephone Usage

> Keep in mind that speaking on the telephone requires better articulation than is necessary in face-to-face conversations.

Remember … there are seven (7) basic ways to address a person you have called on the telephone:

Mr.   Mrs.   Miss   Ma'am   Sir   Ms.   First Name

Always ask about the correct form of address. If the call recipient suggests the use of his or her first name, it is then acceptable for you to do so. Use of a first name may also be acceptable (but not always) when:

- You have established a good rapport over a period of time.
- You have been called by your first name.
- You know the person, and know he/she is comfortable with a first-name basis.

Five Forbidden Phrases*

Forbidden Phrase	Recommended Response
1. "I don't know."	1. "Gee, that's a good question. Let me check and find out."
2. "Just a second."	2. "It may take me a few minutes to get that information. Are you able to hold while I check on that?"
3. "No."	3. "I haven't done that yet?"
4. "We can't do that."	4. "That's a tough one. Let me see what I can do."
5. "You'll have to …"	5. "Here's how we can help with that."

---

* From "Telephone Skills from A – Z," *The Telephone "Doctor" Phone Book* by Nancy Friedman, p. 21-22

Telephone Tips

1. If you dial a wrong number, apologize and hang up.
2. Do not eat, drink, smoke or shuffle papers when on the phone.
3. Speak directly into the mouthpiece.
4. Smile when answering a call and speaking on the phone. Smiling as you answer the phone is reflected in your tone of voice.
5. Avoid making personal phone calls at work.
6. When answering a call, identify yourself and your organization.

Exercise – Telephone Quiz

Directions: Circle either T for True or F for False

T	F	1.	Workplace etiquette means being as professional over the telephone as you are in person.
T	F	2.	It is okay to keep someone waiting on the phone while you are attending to another equally important task.
T	F	3.	You should identify yourself by name when answering a business-related telephone call.
T	F	4.	It is acceptable to make personal calls to your friends at work.
T	F	5.	When you are upset, it is possible to communicate a negative attitude over the phone without realizing it.
T	F	6.	If a caller is rude, it is your right to be equally rude.

(Answers on page 93)

NOTES

Cell Phones

- Turn off your cell phone before entering a concert hall, theater, restaurant, church, any paid entertainment event, or religious ceremony.

- Keep your cell phone conversations innocent enough to withstand being overheard by a third party.

- Realize that walking down the street while talking on a cell phone looks silly to others and it can also be dangerous because it diverts your attention away from what's going on around you.

Voice Mail

If your organization has an automated telephone system, and the attendant's voice is robotic and stilted, consider replacing the automated message with a personal recording. Create your own greeting rather than use the script and voice that comes with the system. Write and record a professional greeting for your own voice mail box. Be sure to let your personality come through when you record (and yes, smile). Put some thought and effort into what you say and how you say it. Keep it short, about 10 to 12 seconds in length. Put some style into it, but keep it professional.

Review your recording. Then record it over and over again, until you sound conversational, just as though you were speaking face-to-face with another person. Don't forget to smile all the way through your recording. No one wants to listen to a bored-sounding voice. Remember, you're representing yourself as well as your organization, so make it good!

Since about 70% of business phone calls contain one-way information, voice mail is an ideal tool. The trick is to use it well. Here are a few suggestions:

1. In most cases when calling a company's main phone number, you can press "0" when you hear the recorded phone-answering message and bypass the automated attendant. Doing so overrides the robotic message and sends your call to a real person, usually the company receptionist. Or, if you know the extension number of the person you are calling, you can press it right away; this will send your call immediately to the person you are calling.

2. Expect your called party not to be available. Have your voice mail message planned out in advance, and keep it brief. Only 25% of business calls reach their intended party on the first try, so be ready to leave a message.

3. Be friendly, and smile while you're recording your message.

4. Speak your message. Don't sound like you're reading it. Compose your messages for the ear, not the eye. Use contractions. For example, rather than "I will be calling you," say "I'll be calling you."

5. Request a specific call-back time. "I need to hear from you by 4:00 P.M. or before." Avoid requests such as, "Call me as soon as you can," or "When you have a few minutes." For best results, be specific.

6. Return business telephone calls within 24 to 48 hours, whether the needs are pressing or not.

Voice Mail Tips
1. Always be prepared to leave a message.
2. The best messages are short ones. Don't ramble.
3. If you must leave a lengthy message, be sure to play it back for accuracy if you can.
4. Never leave a harsh, negative message on voice mail.
5. Don't record anything that can be misinterpreted or that is very confidential.
6. Be sure to check your voice mail at least twice a day.
7. Compliments are some of the nicest messages to receive on voice mail.

E-Mail Etiquette (Netiquette)

E-mail is really just another method of writing a letter, memo, or note. When e-mailing, remember the following:

1. **Assume the messages you send and receive are permanent and public.** Don't say anything in electronic mail that you would not want to be made public or forwarded to others. When a message is sent from an electronic business address, it is considered a business document, and business communications are always subject to scrutiny.

2. **DO NOT USE ALL CAPS**. This is the online version of SHOUTING! Don't use a string of capital letters in your correspondence unless absolutely necessary. Use normal upper- and lower-case letters. TURN OFF THE CAPS LOCK!

3. **Don't send an attachment without including in the body of the text the name of the file** and the reason it should be opened. E-mail viruses spread almost exclusively through attachments.

4. **Don't assume** that the recipient of your message has all of the same computer programs that you do. It is very frustrating to get attachments that you cannot convert into something usable.

5. **Be concise**. E-mail was meant to be one of the quickest ways to communicate. It is much more informal than a letter or even a phone call. Some people receive hundreds of e-mails a day, so keep e-mails short and to the point.

6. **Remember that good grammar and proper language still matter**. Sloppy writing in an e-mail does not make a good impression. On the Internet, the only measure people have to gauge who you are is how you represent yourself electronically. So use the spell-check feature, and double check your grammar and punctuation before sending your e-mails. Complete sentences are always appreciated.

7. **Avoid "flames" and hot buttons**. These are inflammatory or critical messages. Avoid sending junk e-mails, e-mails with insufficient information or any other e-mail that might trigger an upsetting response from the recipient. Also, remember that anyone can forward your message to someone else, so be careful what you say!

8. **Sign your e-mail**. The sender of an e-mail is not always apparent to the recipient simply by looking at the sender's address. It is good practice to sign your e-mail with your name and company information, if applicable. You may want to include your e-mail address as well. Most e-mail services allow you to add a signature that can automatically be attached to each message you send.

9. **Do not repeat messages**. Sending the same e-mail to the same recipient more than once can be perceived as pestering. It is courteous to give recipients a chance to respond to previous messages before re-sending the original message. Many people send and receive e-mail only at regularly scheduled times of the day.

10. **Be brief.** Too much information in one message is a burden on your recipients. Bear in mind that computer screens are harder to read than words on paper.

11. **Include the topic of your message in the subject area.** Clear subject headings make everyone's lives easier.

12. **Don't overuse distribution lists.** When you're sending a message to many people, a long delivery list may appear at the top of the message. This can annoy readers. It also can make your message seem like junk mail.

13. **Understand that "REPLY TO ALL" will go to everyone**. When replying to an e-mail from a distribution list, don't push the REPLY TO ALL button unless you really want your response to go to everyone.

14. **Avoid spamming**. Spam, when used in reference to e-mail, denotes electronic junk mail. Sending junk e-mail (such as an advertisement) using a news group or a mailing list, or sending to people you don't know, is considered "spamming." Avoid this annoying practice. Many spam recipients may retaliate by sending you a flame, or worse by spamming you!

15. **Don't get too informal in work e-mail**. Just because you are sending an e-mail instead of a memo or telephone call doesn't mean you should let your professional standards relax. Although a touch of humor in the tone of an e-mail can be fine, make sure to preserve your professionalism. Although "smileys" may be helpful in social e-mails, try to avoid them in business.

16. **Remember the human side.** The electronic medium may be impersonal, but the receiver is not. Adhere to the same standards of behavior on-line that you follow in real life. If you wouldn't say what you have written in an e-mail, don't send it. Avoid trivial or unnecessary responses to e-mails. It is not necessary to reply to every e-mail you receive.

Chapter 9

POLITICAL SAVVY

POLITICAL SAVVY

Hot Buttons—Handling Anger

Hot buttons are those words or actions that touch a nerve and cause you to become upset and/or lose your temper. People who push your hot buttons can do so unintentionally or intentionally, but the impact is the same—you get angry.

Professional presence means having credibility. We need others to trust us and to feel that our behavior is predictable. It's hard to trust or depend on someone who seems emotionally unstable and shows it through erratic gestures and uncontrolled outbursts.

Know your anger triggers. Awareness can then lead to more responsible reactions.

Some Common Anger Triggers

1. Having a boss or coworker regularly criticize your appearance.
2. Having someone else take credit for your work.
3. Being unfairly criticized without the opportunity to respond.
4. Being deliberately lied to.
5. Discourteous treatment.
6. Watching a coworker show blatant disregard for company rules.
7. Dealing with someone who constantly interrupts you in meetings and conversations.
8. Listening to endless chatter about subjects not related to business.
9. Having a confidence betrayed.
10. Having someone make you look uninformed or stupid in front of others.

Know what pushes your hot buttons, so you can be prepared to act, not react. In that way, you will be better able to manage your relations with others. Some techniques for immediately dealing with hot buttons include:

- Taking a deep breath.
- Excusing yourself to cool off.
- Confirming what you saw or heard by asking the speaker to repeat or clarify what he/she said.
- Paraphrasing, summarizing, or restating the comment.
- Avoiding evaluative communication.
- Respond by using "I" statements, e.g., "When you said that, I heard and felt _____."

EXERCISE – Identifying Your Hot Buttons (Anger Triggers)

Directions: What words or actions push your hot buttons and how do you usually react?

Word/Behavior	Your Reactions	What Could You Do Instead?
1.		
2.		
3.		
4.		

When You Are on the Receiving End of Anger or Criticism

Professionalism is often defined as grace under pressure. In every business person's life, there comes a time when he or she suffers some type of business humiliation. Depending on the organization, it may happen more than once. There are a number of ways to react, most of which just worsen the problem.

Here is a list of ways not to react to criticism:

1. Don't make excuses. "I haven't been feeling well lately, and you just keep making me work late. It's no wonder that I botched that project, I'm just exhausted."

2. Don't cry and become defensive. "I know you don't like me. You have never taken me or my work seriously. You love to humiliate me in front of the office and make me cry."

3. Don't counterattack. "Well, I may not have gotten this report in on time, but at least I didn't get drunk and make a fool of myself at the last office party!"

Some Ways to React to Criticism*:

1. Allow yourself to feel anger, and don't bury or deny it. Use moans and groans, grumbles and tears, but do it privately.

2. Look at the situation from a different perspective. Can it be interpreted differently?

3. Build your own logical arguments as to why your reaction is justified and write it down. Be active—pace, shout, hit a pillow, meditate, exercise, say a prayer—but again, do it privately.

4. Change your environment. Have a safe place where you can retreat and be alone. Engage in a pre-planned activity such as exercising, playing a game, watching a funny video, or reading a funny or inspiring book.

---

* Adapted from *The Manager's Pocket Guide to Emotional Intelligence*, Emily A. Sterett, Ph.D. (HRD Press, Amherst, MA 2000)

When You Are Attacked Publicly

One of the best strategies for dealing with a situation in which you feel you have very little control is to use nonverbal behavior. If someone confronts you during a presentation in a meeting, look the person squarely in the eye, maintain eye contact for a moment, then look away. That way, your message becomes, "I heard you, but what you are saying is so off-track and uncalled for that I choose not to deal with it." This will help you keep control of the situation and actually enhances your power.

Reacting without having time to construct your case can be a mistake. Why get dragged into an unfriendly arena? In the heat of the moment, the less said the better. Showing little or no reaction can actually take the wind out of an angry sail, and you will end up the better player, having displayed more poise and presence. You can always reintroduce the issue later, between just the two of you, when tempers are more under control.

If a colleague or even a superior has criticized you in public, it is always possible to take him or her aside later and quietly say: "Please don't criticize me in public. If you have any criticism to make, tell me about it privately." Most bullies are so taken aback by a straightforward approach that they often change their behavior immediately.

Think First, Act Later

Remember attackers are out of control in the first place, and you don't need to contribute to their negative behavior or play by their rules by succumbing to pressure. Your best strategy is to maintain control over yourself and your territory. You can do this by taking the following steps:

1. Analyze the conflict from the perspective of both sides.
2. Create distance in time and space between your attacker and you.
3. Know your own vulnerable spots and weaknesses.
4. Determine your best- and worst-case scenarios for action.
5. Develop a plan for responding to an attack and stick to it.
6. Remain confident that you will succeed, despite your attacker.
7. Establish allies among your coworkers.

Self-Control

Self-control is defined as "keeping disruptive emotions and impulses in check." It is:

- Thinking clearly and staying focused under pressure.
- Staying composed, positive, and unflappable even in trying moments.
- Managing impulsive feelings and distressing emotions.

Workplace Social Functions

Social functions are very important within organizations. Make every effort to attend your company's holiday parties, picnics, and departmental gatherings. A lot of information is exchanged informally in these settings. By attending social functions, you:

- Give others the impression that you are a team player.
- Get the opportunity to network.
- Get to meet the important people within your organization.

Office Social No-No's

1. Not showing up. You may leave early, but you need to attend. Make your entrance no later than 15 minutes after the time on the invitation.

2. Ignoring your boss.

3. Gossiping about your boss or co-workers.

4. Overeating and over-drinking.

5. Flirting with a coworker.

6. Losing your cool, showing anger.

7. Missing the "big moment" (the reason for the event).

8. Believing that you can make a fool of yourself and everyone will forgive and forget.

9. Not dressing appropriately for the occasion (too casual or too dressy).

10. Cheating in sports events (golf, softball, tennis, etc.).

11. Eating over the buffet.

12. Being too loud and making yourself the center of attention.

13. Clustering with friends and not mingling with others.

Office Politics

Office politics are the strategies that people in organizations use to gain or maintain a competitive advantage. Just as organizations require strategic planning, tactics, and maneuvers, your career requires these same elements. It is difficult to move forward in any organization without engaging in some form of office politics.

Your Choices

Most people who go out of their way to avoid office politics will find themselves frustrated, angry, and out of the loop. There are, however, many ways to deal with office politics.

At the lowest level of office politics, you can engage in several activities without considering yourself "a political person." The following activities can provide a positive boost to your career development:

- Relationship building
- Networking
- Team involvement
- Persuasive communications

At the next level of office politics, you may go beyond the basics of career advancement and include the following:

- Using negotiating tactics
- Making yourself known and visible
- Self-promotion
- Seeking additional responsibility
- Information gathering
- Maintaining emotional self-control
- Projecting a successful image
- Knowing your competition
- Cultivating organizational resources
- Obtaining access to top executives
- Developing advanced communication skills
- Volunteering for important projects
- Complimenting and supporting decision makers
- Maintaining confidence
- Developing a following

At the highest level of political engagement (that of real power and control), you may also engage in the following:

- Cultivating influential relationships outside the organization
- Socializing with influential people
- Modeling your behaviors and appearances after the best in the organization
- Always controlling your behavior
- Becoming an expert in your field
- Making things happen
- Leaving nothing to chance

All of the above behaviors are considered legitimate and ethical inside and outside the business world. However, when playing office politics moves into the realm of lies and deception, you risk losing your own sense of morality and ethics.

Recognizing Devious Office Tactics

Office politics can also be played in a devious and hurtful manner. Watch out for people who use the following tactics:

- *False Support*—Deliberately giving you false encouragement and bad advice, which you act upon to your detriment.
- *Bad-mouthing*—Making damaging statements about you, raising questions about your ability to work on a project, or raising false concerns about your credibility.
- *Back-stabbing*—Falsely befriending you by appearing very nice, but secretly ruining your image and career.
- *Stealing Ideas*—Taking your good ideas and passing them off as their own.
- *Crippling*—Undermining and destroying your self-confidence with a steady stream of put-downs, negative comments, and statements that lead you to believe others do not like you.
- *Emotional Blackmail*—Threatening to disclose something you have done that will make you look bad or ruin your career if it were brought out into the open.
- *Zoning*—Creating dissension between you and other people in the workplace in order to gain power and control over you.
- *Railroading*—Making conditions so miserable that you are forced to leave.

Office Politics—Principles to Follow

1. Thoroughly understand your job, corporate culture, and system.
2. Stay focused and have solid goals.
3. Remain flexible and positive.
4. Know when to hold and when to fold, i.e., pick your fights wisely.
5. Be a team player. Play fair.
6. Learn to communicate effectively.
7. Be proactive and not reactive.
8. Think first, act later.
9. Be responsible and productive.
10. Build solid relationships.

Exercise – Political Savvy Quiz*

Multiple Choice—Choose the Best Answer

1. It's late Thursday afternoon. Your boss is working on a rush project that's due Friday morning. She mentions that she will be working late this evening, but doesn't ask for help. You have very tentative plans to go to a movie with a friend. You decide to:

   A. Say nothing and leave at your usual time.

   B. Say that you wish you could stay and help her, but you have plans for the evening.

   C. Tell her that you have plans but would be happy to break them to stay and help her.

   D. Say nothing about your plans; ask her what you can do to help.

2. At the end of a very frustrating day, you and your supervisor become involved in a very heated discussion over a work-related issue. You know you are right, but he says you're wrong. You lose your temper, raise your voice, and finally storm out of his office. Since it is quitting time, you immediately leave for the day. The next day, you:

   A. Pretend that nothing happened.

   B. Stay very cool, and wait for the supervisor to make the first move.

   C. Go to see him as soon as possible to apologize for losing your temper and storming out of the office.

3. On the morning of a big presentation to a senior executive, you wake up with a sore throat, a headache, and a slight fever. You know you are coming down with the cold that's been going around the office. You have been preparing for this presentation for three months, and it has taken one month just to get on the executive's calendar. You know your boss can give the presentation because you have practiced before her three times and she has the Power Point presentation. You decide to:

   A. Call your boss, explain the situation to her, and let her decide whether you should come to work.

   B. Go to work, give the presentation, and say nothing about your illness until later.

   C. Call in sick, because you know you'll only get worse if you go out.

4. Your office has two social functions a year: a picnic in the summer and a holiday party at the end of the year. You dislike picnics and rarely go to them, even with your best friends and family, because you hate the way you look in picnic clothes, you sunburn very easily, and you don't like insects. The office picnic is tomorrow, you decide to:

   A. Go to the picnic late and leave early.

   B. Go to the picnic and try to enjoy it. *Team player*

   C. Request annual leave for the day, saying something has come up.

   D. Explain to your boss why you don't want to go to the picnic and offer to stay and answer the phones.

* The Political Savvy Quiz and Tips are the work of Tim Stranges of The Timothy Group, Rockville, Maryland, and are included with his kind permission.

5. Your old boss moves to a new position and you apply for her old job. You are not chosen for the job, instead someone who you think is much less qualified gets it. You try to work for the new boss, but find it difficult to do so because of your perception of his inadequacies. You decide to:

   A. Using very subtle means, make him look bad whenever possible in the hope that upper level management will see his inadequacies.

   B. Continue to do your job and avoid him as much as possible.

   C. Try to find out why management chose him over you, and if it is because of your own weaknesses, work to overcome them. *Developmental needs*

   D. Find a new job.

6. You are one of five professionals in a division. Right now all five of you have outside offices with windows. You are being moved to new space that has only four outside offices and one inside office. Everyone wants an outside office and the others are very vocal about it. Your supervisor doesn't know what to do. You:

   A. Stand up for your "rights" and continue arguing for outside space.

   B. Volunteer to take the inside space.

   C. Suggest to the supervisor that she assign the offices based on seniority (knowing that you are the most senior person).

   D. Suggest to the supervisor that the five of you draw straws for the space.

7. A new employee who uses a wheelchair is hired in your branch. Your office has a practice of going out for lunch to nearby restaurants once a month to celebrate birthdays. You invite your new co-worker to the next luncheon, but she declines. You continue to invite her for the next several months, but she always has an excuse. By this time you feel you know her well enough to ask her why she doesn't go. She tells you the restaurants you go to are not accessible. You:

   A. Tell her you're sorry she can't join you, and continue the luncheons.

   B. Tell her that it's not fair and that you're going to talk to your co-workers about boycotting the restaurants and discontinuing the luncheons.

   C. Tell her you're sorry, then find an accessible restaurant for the next luncheon and surprise her with the good news.

   D. Ask her if there are any nearby restaurants she likes that are accessible, and if so, would she like to go there next time.

8. It's 2:00 on Friday afternoon. You have been working on one major project all week and expect to be finished in a half hour. The project isn't due until the middle of next week. Your boss comes running in with a "rush" that he wants completed by 5:00. You know it will take only one hour to do it. You decide to:

   A. Hold off working on the "rush" for a half hour until you are able to finish the major project.

   B. Put your project aside and begin working on the "rush" project immediately.

9.   You complete your boss's "rush" project and give it to the secretary for typing into final. She completes her job and returns it to you for final proofing and initialing. It's 4:00 and the rush is due at 5:00. You decide not to proof it, but instead just initial it and hand-carry it to your boss. He discovers several grammatical errors and returns it to you. You:

   A. Apologize and say you will do your best to make sure it doesn't happen again.

   B. Tell him you didn't proof it because he wanted it in such a hurry.

   C. Tell him that the secretary should have caught the errors.

10.   You have been selected for a prestigious training class that is being held at a site about one mile from your office. Classroom hours for this program are from 8:00 A.M. to 4:30 P.M. and do not coincide with your normal work hours of 7:00 A.M. to 3:30 P.M. You normally commute to your job by car pool, but you could drive yourself to the class site, which would require additional time and expense. You decide to:

   A. Continue taking your car pool and, with apologies to the instructor, leave class early everyday.

   B. Make other transportation arrangements to allow you to attend the entire class every day.

11.   This same prestigious training class lasts an entire week. You finished all critical work products before you left for the training, and your boss arranged for a co-worker to cover for you, but you fear that some unexpected crises may come up. You decide to:

   A. Call the office every day and try to stop by at least once during the week.

   B. Call the office in the middle of the week to see how things are going.

   C. Not worry about the crises. Your co-worker and boss can handle them.

12.   You have just gotten a promotion to a new job in a new office where the supervisor and about half of the staff work from 9:00 A.M. to 5:30 P.M. The other employees work earlier hours. At your old office, which is only a mile away, you were in a carpool whose members worked from 7:00 A.M. to 3:30 P.M. You live far from the office, where there is no public transportation. You decide to:

   A. Stay in your old carpool and tell your supervisor that you need to work from 7:00 A.M. to 3:30 P.M. because you live so far away and commuting is hard.

   B. Explain your situation to your supervisor and ask her if you can stay in your old carpool and work your old hours.

   C. Explain your situation to your supervisor and ask her if you can work your old hours until you are able to get into a later carpool in one or two months.

   D. Start working from 9:00 A.M. to 5:30 P.M. immediately and drive by yourself until you are able to get into a later carpool.

13. In your new office, you quickly discover that an intra-office battle is going on between one small faction headed by your supervisor and another large faction consisting of three-fourths of the employees. It is so bad that the two sides rarely speak to each other. The large faction of employees has asked you to join them in their fight against the supervisor. You:

A. Tell them you can't join their group because you owe allegiance to the supervisor who hired/promoted you into your new job.

B. Tell them you can't join their group until you have had time to investigate the issues and ask them to give you a month to make up your mind.

C. Join their group because you decide that three-fourths of the employees can't be wrong.

(D.) Tell them that you are so new you want to remain neutral. *Try*

loyalty to person who brought you in

14. A new employee who has cerebral palsy is hired in your office. He has severe muscle spasms that cause him to perspire profusely, thus giving off an offensive odor. He is an excellent worker and has a great personality. Everyone in the office likes him, but they are apprehensive about saying anything to him about the odor, which has become intolerable. You decide that you need to do something, so you:

Disabilities

other options

A. Buy a can of super-strength spray deodorant and write a very nice, polite, anonymous note telling him what a great addition he has been to the office and how he could be even better if he would just use the deodorant.

EAP

(B.) Meet with the employee outside of the office and discuss what you have noticed. Ask him if there is any way to solve the problem. Tell him you are available to assist him if he would like assistance.

C. Go to his work space, gently tell him about the odor problem, and give him a can of the super-strength deodorant that you use every day because you have an odor problem, too.

15. A management intern has an opportunity to go on a 30-day detail to his organization's headquarters office in Washington, D.C. While he is there, he will work with the key executives of the organization, most of whom are conservative in their manners and dress. This intern has worn a large gold earring for the last five years. Although he got a lot of grief from co-workers when he first put it on, and is still referred to by some as the "pirate," most of them are used to it now. When he goes on his detail to headquarters, he should:

A. Wear a small stud rather than the large earring.

B. Not wear the large earring for the first two weeks until people get to know him, then wear it the last two weeks.

(C.) Not wear any earring while he is on detail to headquarters.

D. Wear the large earring and when he notices people staring at it, explain to them why he wears it.

(Answers on page 93)

Political Savvy (Information is Power)

Exercise: Answer the following questions with the people your organization in mind:

1. Who does what job in your organization?

2. Who seems to command influence and respect?

3. Who seems to be "in the loop"—that is, who communicates with upper levels of management frequently and effectively?

4. Who is climbing the corporate ladder?

5. Who is frequently called upon to answer questions?

6. Who is frequently quoted?

7. Who makes the key decisions?

8. Who writes the significant memos?

9. Who runs the meetings?

Once you identify the people associated with the questions above, get to know them and cultivate them as your primary sources of information and aid. However, you must also identify something you can give them in return for that information and help. One thing you can always give is your interest. For example, ask for a conversation rather than help or information. Say:

- "I would like a chance to speak with you."
- "When is a good time to talk about this?"
- "Mind if I pick your brain?"
- "I need to find out more, and I would really like to talk to you about it. What is a convenient time for you?"

The Office Grapevine

- Is an informal workplace communication network for news and gossip.
- You cannot get rid of it, so you'd better tune in on it.
- Is usually over 80% accurate.
- You can learn valuable information from it.
- You can use it to assess the organization's priorities.
- Makes it easier for you to maintain a professional presence when you know what's going on in the office.

Political Savvy Tips

1.   Know the culture and values of your organization, the written and unwritten rules regarding dress, appearance, working and lunch hours, office/desk appearance, use of humor, attendance at social functions, etc.

2.   Learn how to operate within the political environment—not Democrat or Republican politics, but office politics. What are the priorities of your organization? How can you help the organization meet those priorities?

3.   Learn who has power within your organization. How did they get it? How do they hold on to it? Who are the up-and-comers? How did they become up-and-comers? What can you do to become one? Don't forget that you may need to blow your own horn if you want to be heard (but don't blow it too loudly).

4.   Learn the difference between formal and informal power. Understand the power that secretaries and executive assistants can have. Treat everyone with respect, especially those in support or assistant positions.

5.   Try to see the world through your boss's eyes. Understand that your boss has pressures, too. Make his or her job easier by giving them more than they ask for and even anticipating their requests. Be loyal to your boss.

6.   Pay attention to the image you project. Maintain a positive, can-do attitude. Display self-confidence but don't be arrogant. Take pride in all your work. Pay attention to detail. Demonstrate integrity and keep your word. Set the example.

7.   Be flexible. Don't become upset when priorities change. Volunteer for new projects, especially those that will provide new challenges. Be willing to take appropriate risks and to make sacrifices. Strive to learn new things.

8.   Ask for and accept constructive feedback willingly. Listen to what's being said and repeat it back to make sure you have understood properly. Don't become defensive. Discuss what steps you can take to correct the identified deficiency.

9.   Find a mentor, coach, or sponsor who can help you climb the ladder of success. Ask your boss for suggestions, and if he/she can't think of anyone, then ask his/her manager. You can also ask the head of human resources and/or the head of your company's equal opportunity department for suggestions. Make sure the proposed mentor is well-respected in the organization and that there is a good fit between you and him/her.

10. Strive for excellence.

> ## Avoid negative wording that references other cultures, such as:
> - To Welsh
> - To Jew Down
> - Dutch Treat
> - Street Arab
> - Indian Giver
> - Yellow Peril

Networking

Networking is a skill that has been around since humans have been bartering. People have always used their contacts to get what they wanted. Networking is the personal process of linking with others to exchange information, achieve a goal, receive advice, meet key contacts, and gain access to resources. Networking occurs when, for example, you ask someone where they bought their computer or if they know of a good speaker or trainer, or tell an associate about a job opening. Networking is an organized method of making links from people you know to the people they know, and of gaining and using an ever-expanding base of contacts. Many say it is comparable to the office grapevine, the "good ole boys network," or the "women's network."

Networking is about who knows you, not who you know.

Basic Networking Guidelines*

1. Be open-minded – Don't stereotype people or prejudge their long-term value.
2. Be prepared – Make sure you have business cards, brochures, and know what you want.
3. Take the time to network and cultivate new relationships – Understand that networking is about building rapport first, not selling.
4. Treat those in your network as equals – Choose network members based on information, not position.
5. Don't be afraid to ask, but do not be overly demanding.
6. Reciprocate the favor – If you ask for a favor, offer to return the favor and follow through if the other person asks something in return. If a person did you a favor in the past, you are duty-bound to help them.
7. Don't feel guilty about rejecting a request that is illegal, unethical, or immoral.
8. Give without expectations – Realize a return favor may not come back to you.
9. Follow up with a thank-you note – Always express your appreciation, regardless of whether your expectations have been met. When someone has helped you, tell the person the outcome of the help when you thank them.
10. Accept rejection gracefully – Recognize that rejection will occur. Thank the person regardless for spending the time to talk with you and move on.

Business Cards

Business cards are a part of your overall professional presence.

- Always carry business cards and keep them in a convenient place.
- Invest in a professional-looking card.
- Never give someone a card with crossed-out phone numbers or addresses numbers or one that is ripped or dirty.
- Exchange business cards at the beginning of a meeting, preferably the moment you sit down and before serious discussion begins.
- Exchange cards before or after a meal, not while people are eating.
- Present your card face up and turned so that the person receiving the card can read it immediately.

* From *Is Your "Net" Working?: A Complete Guide to Building Contacts and Career Visibility,* Anne Boe and Bettie B. Youngs, pp. 9-20.

Exercise: Identifying Your Networks

Under each category below, identify five people and/or organizations that comprise your networks:

1. Work/Business   Suppo, Susan, Hetzel

2. Family/Extended Family

3. Friends

4. Clubs/Professional Organizations

5. Athletics/Sports Organizations

If you have none to list, it's time for you to start networking! List two people you could benefit from by knowing better, two organizations you could join, and two activities that you could use to network.

Appendix

Resources (Bibliography)

1. *The Book of Etiquette*, Michael MacFarlane, Sterling Publishing, New York, NY, 2004.

2. *Business Etiquette and Professionalism*, M. Kay duPont, Crisp Publications, Menlo Park, CA, 1990.

3. *Commonsense Etiquette*, Marjabelle Young Stewart and Elizabeth Lawrence, St. Martins Press, New York, NY, 1999.

4. *Curious Customs*, Tad Tuleja, Crown Publishers, New York, NY, 1987.

5. *Emily Post on Etiquette* (Revised Edition), Elizabeth Post, Harper Collins Publishers, New York, NY, 1995.

6. *The Etiquette Advantage*, June Hines Moore, Boardman & Holman, Nashville, TN, 1998.

7. *Etiquette for Dummies*, Sue Fox, Wiley Publishing, New York, NY, 1999.

8. *The Everything Etiquette Book*, Nat Segaloff, Adams Media Corp., Avon, MA, 1998.

9. *First Impression, Best Impression*, Janet Elsea, Simon & Schuster, New York, NY, 1985.

10. *Hot Buttons, How to Resolve Conflict and Cool Everyone Down*, Sybil Evans and Sherry Suib Cohen, Harper Collins Publishers, New York, NY, 2000.

11. *How To Behave: A Guide to Modern Manners for the Socially Challenged*, Caroline Tiger, Quirk Productions, Philadelphia, PA, 2003.

12. *Is Your "Net" Working?*, Anne Boe and Bettie B. Youngs, John Wiley & Sons, New York, NY, 1989.

13. *Language Customs and Protocol*, Herff I. Moore, L. Rex Olicer, and Deborah L. Veady, Crisp Publications, Menlo Park, CA, 1992.

14. *The Little Book of Etiquette, Tips for Socially Correct Dining*, Sheila M. Long, Barnes & Noble, New York, NY, 2000.

15. *The Manager's Pocket Guide to Emotional Intelligence*, Emily A. Sterrett, HRD Press, Amherst, MA, 2000.

16. *Managing Anger*, Rebecca R. Luhn, Crisp Publications, Menlo Park, CA, 1992.

17. *Miss Manner's Guide for the Turn-of-the-Millennium*, Judith Martin, Simon & Schuster, New York, NY, 1989.

18. *Office Politics*, Rebecca Luhn Wolfe, Crisp Publications, Menlo Park, CA, 1997.

19. *The Professional Image*, Susan Bixler, The Putman Publishing Group, New York, NY, 1984.

20. *Professional Presence*, Susan Bixler, The Putman Publishing Group, New York, NY, 1991.

21. *The Silent Language*, Edward T. Hall, Fawcett World Library, New York, NY, 1969.

22. *Telephone Skills from A to Z*, Nancy J. Friedman, Crisp Publications, Menlo Park, CA, 1995.

23. *Winning at Office Politics*, Andrew DuBrin, Prentice Hall, Engelwood Cliffs, NJ, 1990.

Answer Keys

What Do You Know Before We Begin Quiz - Pages 3 & 4

1.	T	14.	F	27.	T	40.	F
2.	T	15.	T	28.	F	41.	T
3.	T	16.	T	29.	T	42.	F
4.	T	17.	T	30.	T	43.	F
5.	F	18.	F	31.	T	44.	T
6.	F	19.	F	32.	T	45.	T
7.	F	20.	T	33.	T	46.	T
8.	T	21.	T	34.	T	47.	T
9.	T	22.	T	35.	T	48.	T
10.	F	23.	T	36.	F	49.	T
11.	T	24.	F	37.	F	50.	F
12.	T	25.	T	38.	F		
13.	T	26.	T	39.	T		

If your total score is 44 or above, you have well-developed sense of workplace etiquette and will be able to use this book to reinforce many of the things you are currently doing as well as fine-tune other skills.

If your score is 38 - 43, you know many of the basics of workplace etiquette. This book will help you identify and understand the more important or complex issues essential to developing and enhancing your workplace etiquette.

If your total score is less than 38, this book will provide you with the basics and an understanding of the more advanced skills of workplace etiquette.

Regardless of your score, please go back and retake the quiz after you have finished this book and compare your scores.

Etiquette Basics Quiz - Page 19

1.	T
2.	T
3.	T
4.	T
5.	T
6.	T
7.	T
8.	T
9.	T
10.	F

Meeting and Greeting Quiz - Page 29

1. B
2. B
3. B
4. C
5. A

Dining Ettiquette Quiz - Page 46

1. T	11. T
2. T	12. F
3. F	13. T
4. F	14. T
5. F	15. T
6. T	16. F
7. T	17. T
8. T	18. T
9. T	19. T
10. T	20. T

Nonverbal Feedback - Page 58

1. Attentive, willing to listen
2. Closed-minded, not listening
3. Bewildered, frustrated
4. Bored
5. Interested, friendly
6. Closed-minded, disapproving
7. Attentive listening
8. Bored, impatient, not listening
9. Bored, impatient, not listening
10. Bored, impatient, not listening

Telephone Quiz - Page 70

1. T
2. F
3. T
4. F
5. T
6. F

Political Savvy Quiz - Pages 83 - 86

1. D	6. B	11. A
2. C	7. D	12. D
3. B	8. B	13. A
4. B	9. A	14. B
5. C	10. B	15. C

Index

Breinigsville, PA USA
08 March 2011
257155BV00004B/1/P

9 780982 383100